Rockhounding California

Help Us Keep This Guide Up to Date

Every effort has been made by the author and editors to make this guide as accurate and useful as possible. However, many things can change after a guide is published—roads are detoured, phone numbers change, facilities come under new management, etc.

We would love to hear from you concerning your experiences with this guide and how you feel it could be improved and kept up to date. While we may not be able to respond to all comments and suggestions, we'll take them to heart and we'll also make certain to share them with the author. Please send your comments and suggestions to the following address:

Globe Pequot Press
Reader Response/Editorial Department
P.O. Box 480
Guilford, CT 06437

Or you may e-mail us at:

editorial@GlobePequot.com

Thanks for your input, and happy rockhounding!

Rockhounding California

A Guide to the State's Best Rockhounding Sites

Second Edition

Gail A. Butler

Updated by Members of the California Federation of
Mineralogical Societies, compiled by Shep Koss

FALCON GUIDES

GUILFORD, CONNECTICUT
HELENA, MONTANA

To buy books in quantity for corporate use
or incentives, call **(800) 962–0973**
or e-mail **premiums@GlobePequot.com**.

FALCONGUIDES®

Copyright © 1995, 2012 Morris Book Publishing, LLC
Previous edition published by Falcon Publishing, Inc., 1995

FalconGuides is an imprint of Globe Pequot Press.
Falcon, FalconGuides, and Outfit Your Mind are registered trademarks of Morris Book Publishing, LLC.

Consulting editor, first edition: W. R. C. Shedenhelm

Library of Congress Cataloging-in-Publication data is available on file.

ISBN 978-0-7627-7141-7

Printed in the United States of America
10 9 8 7 6 5 4 3 2 1

Contents

Rockhounding Sites in Southern California

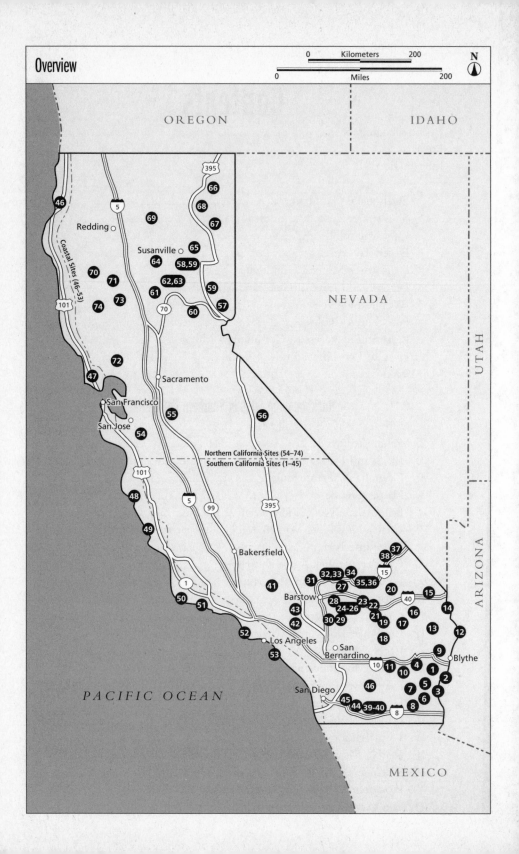

Overview

Kilometers
0   200

Miles
0   200

N

OREGON   IDAHO

Coastal Sites (46–53)

Redding

Susanville

Sacramento

San Francisco

San Jose

NEVADA

UTAH

Northern California Sites (54–74)
Southern California Sites (1–45)

Bakersfield

Barstow

Los Angeles

San Bernardino

San Diego

PACIFIC OCEAN

ARIZONA

Blythe

MEXICO

Rockhounding Sites in Coastal California

Rockhounding Sites in Northern California

Acknowledgments

There are many people who have made the writing of this book possible. To list all of them would require another whole volume. So I will start at the beginning and be as brief as possible.

I thank my grandfather, Alvin B. Butler, a prospector. When I was very young, he nurtured my interest in rockhounding by bringing me wonderful rock and mineral specimens he found on gold prospecting trips.

Thanks to James R. Mitchell for his rockhounding guide, *Gem Trails of California,* which led me on my first trips into the wilderness to look for rocks years ago.

Thanks to the members of the Bear Gulch Rock Club of Ontario, California, who further encouraged my interest in both rockhounding and turning my found stones into lovely lapidary treasures. I am also grateful for their companionship and fun on many rockhounding trips. A special thanks also to member Bob Kawka, who strongly encouraged me to write my first article.

I wish to thank W. R. C. Shedenhelm, editor emeritus of *Rock & Gem* magazine, who published my first article in 1985 and then said, "Keep 'em coming." I also thank him for his ongoing encouragement, humor, winefests, humor, sharing of books and maps, humor, his valuable advice, and of course his humor. It was greatly due to him that this guide was written.

To my mother, Barbara Parry, heartfelt thanks from me, my feline friends, and plants for feeding and watering them while I was gallivanting about the state taking photos and detailing site write-ups for this book. Thanks also for picking up the tons of mail delivered while I was away.

Thank you, thank you to my dear friends and partners, Mo and Ed Hemler, who tracked my gallivantings and were prepared to mount a rescue mission should I not return or check in at the appointed times.

Thank you to Scooter Patrick, mechanic extraordinaire, who kept my Suzuki running in top form. In a year of running about the state, often in the remotest reaches of wilderness by myself, the "Sooz" never failed.

Thank you to my aunt and uncle, Peggy and Ed Butler, who allowed me to use their home as the base from which all the northern sites were collected and for joining me on some of the expeditions. Thank you also to my father, Al Butler, and his betrothed, Sandy Olsen, for more bed and board during my travels.

Thank you to the San Diego Mineral and Gem Society and their junior members for inviting me to accompany them on a trip to one of the sites listed in this guide. I appreciate their ongoing mailings of the *Pegmatite Bulletin,* which contains valuable information regarding legislation that affects rockhounding, some of which has gone into this guide.

Thanks to the members of the Mount Jura Gem and Mineral Club who gave me directions and information for some of the northern sites described in this guide.

Thank you to Nancy and Howard Fisher of Opal Hill Fire Agate Mine for teaching me their techniques of mining for fire agate.

Thanks go to Herman Schob for his company on several of the southern site trips and for the information he sent on some of the northern sites.

Thank you to Jude Kendrick, with whom I discovered and explored some of the desert sites that subsequently ended up in this book.

Thank you to Garret Romaine for the photos and captions he submitted for this edition.

Also very hearty thank-yous to Ed Ferner, Eric Bonzell, Stephan Telm, Robert Verish, Janelle Williams, Jon Lovegren, Stan Bogosian, Anne Schafer, Fred Ott, Jim Brace-Thompson, and Cyndi Mandell—all members of the California Federation of Mineralogical Societies—and CFMS in general for their contributions to the second edition.

Preface

The object of this guide is to provide rockhounds with as much up-to-date information as possible to enable them to collect the many interesting gem and mineral treasures that abound in California.

Many of the gem and mineral guides for California are years, sometimes decades, out of date. Legislation continually changes land status and access to areas in California. New roads have been built, altering directions and mileages to many collecting sites.

In most cases the author has visited the sites listed to check on mileages, status, and availability of collecting material. Several sites were suggested by friends of the author who also enjoy a weekend of rockhounding and have their favorite collecting spots.

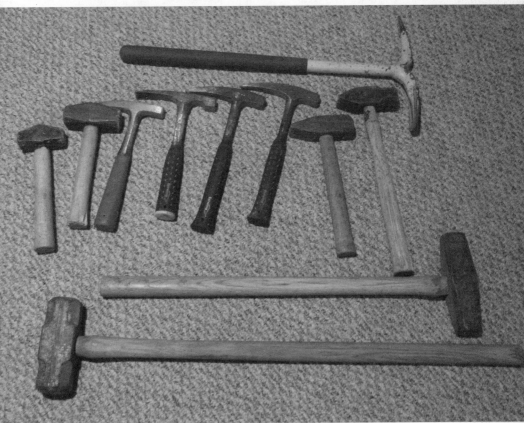

Most rockhounds have a diverse collection of hammers and picks at their disposal.
PHOTO BY GARRET ROMAINE

The information in this guide is presented so that rockhounds and mineral collectors, whether new to the hobby or veterans, will be able to find interesting gems and minerals for their collections and lapidary projects.

By no means does this guide list all the mineral or collecting sites in California. It does list accessible sites the author has enjoyed visiting. These sites also contain a diversity of gem and mineral material. Some sites are included because they are old favorites among rockhounds and are traditional weekend camping and gathering spots. Some were discovered by the author.

Commercial mines are not listed in the site write-ups, as they are not generally accessible to rockhounds. A few that allow occasional collecting are listed under Rockhound Access to Commercial Mines.

Also listed are published sources used in the writing of this guide or which the author feels may be of interest to those who would like more information about rockhounding.

Lastly, this book is dedicated to all rockhounds past, present, and future and to the enjoyable hobby of rockhounding. May it continue!

Introduction

California! Land of earthquakes and wind-driven wildfires, scorching deserts, wave-washed beaches, and breathtaking mountain vistas. If any one word could best describe the state of California, that word would be *variety*. California has something to offer everyone.

Several friendly arguments exist on how California received its name. One favorite is that the name is taken from the words *kali,* meaning "high," and *forno,* meaning "hills." Another argument states that the name comes from the Latin *calida fornax,* which translates to "hot furnace." Still another theory maintains that the Indian word *tchalifalni-al,* roughly meaning "the sandy land against the water," is the true source of California's name. While all these arguments seem plausible enough, the last one appears most reasonable because California has a mostly temperate climate and more than 1,200 miles of coastline.

The name "California" often evokes historic gold rush days and images of crusty, sourdough miners. Gold is, not surprisingly, the state mineral and is still avidly sought on weekends by recreational gold prospectors.

The California poppy, the golden-hued state flower, brightly adorns the hillsides in early spring. The endearing California valley quail, with its curious topknot and white facial markings, is the state bird. Benitoite, a rare, transparent blue crystal found only in California, is the state gemstone.

Although known mostly for its history of gold production, California also yields a wide variety of other valuable mineral commodities. Ghost towns and abandoned mines testify to a rich history of precious metals mining, not only of gold but also copper and silver.

Modern-day mines, some still producing gold, also extract other ores and minerals, such as iron, lead, tungsten, zinc, quicksilver, talc, chromite, and borate minerals.

California is truly a mineralogical wonderland and a virtual haven for rock and gem collectors. Practically every known mineral exists in some quantity somewhere in California.

The Landscape

No single type of terrain can best represent California's geographic and geologic diversity. The state's total landmass is 158,297 square miles.

Moving from the central and southeastern edge of California, westward toward the mighty Pacific Ocean, we first encounter deserts at the southern

Desert flora. Photo by Garret Romaine

end and up into the central portion of the state. These are the Mojave and Colorado Deserts and the infamous Death Valley.

Transverse mountain ranges, so named because they lie contrary to the prevailing northwesterly fabric of the state's landmass, create a barrier to coastal moisture, resulting in these thirsty but austerely beautiful and mineral-rich desert regions.

The northern portion of the state, from a northeastern starting point along the state's border with Nevada and again moving westward toward the sea, consists mostly of sage-covered flatlands and hills giving way to pine-sheathed mountains and rolling, oak-covered hills.

California has forty-one peaks higher than 10,000 feet, the tallest being Mount Whitney at 14,496 feet. The Central Valley, totaling approximately one-fifth of the state's landmass, consists of farms and cultivated land and has little in the way of mineral values.

California can be divided into four basic types of terrain: coastal beaches, alpine mountain or oak-covered hills, inland deserts, and sage-covered flats. Along the 1,200 miles of coast, watchful beachcombers can find tide-washed jade, agate, abalone, and fossilized whalebone. Mountains and oaken-hill regions yield gold, clear and smoky quartz crystals, copper minerals, jade, serpentine, agate, petrified wood, and obsidian. Sage flats and inland areas offer amethyst, obsidian, marble, agate, and fossils. Deserts—often the richest sources of collecting material—yield fossils, agate, geodes, garnet, fire agate, jasper, copper minerals, gold, fluorite, translucent common opal, onyx, turquoise, and more!

Wintertime weather extremes range from below freezing in mountain and desert areas to greater than 120 degrees Fahrenheit in the deserts during summer. Otherwise temperatures are generally moderate statewide. Rainfall can vary from 80 inches in northern coastal regions to nary a drop in the deserts. The mountains average 1 to 8 feet of snow, depending on the location.

Coastal and inland foothills are covered with oak trees and wild oats and in spring are blanketed with California poppy, yellow mustard plant, and purple lupine. The mountains are forested with a variety of conifers and wild ferns, while blackberry brambles, poison oak, and poison ivy are found near creeks and streams. Desert vistas are adorned with the potentially painful cholla cactus (sometimes called jumping cactus), beavertail and barrel cactus, wide expanses of creosote bush, ephedra (Mormon tea), and mallow. Desert washes are silhouetted with mesquite trees, palo verde, and lavender-gray smoke trees.

The geology of the state consists of some of the oldest rocks on Earth. Portions of the San Gabriel Mountain Range in southern California have been dated to 1.7 billion years old.

California's geologic variety is the result of an assortment of processes. Rocks forming the geology of the state have been the product of volcanic, sedimentary, and metamorphic mechanisms. Other ongoing processes continue to etch and chisel the landscape, such as weathering by wind and water. Cycles of drought, alternating with mud flows and landslides caused by prolific rainfall, wildfires, and earthquakes, continue to change and sculpt the landscape in dramatic ways. All have served to form and fashion California into a geologic wonderland. As a result of these many dynamic processes, a great abundance of mineral and gem material awaits the eager rockhound.

The majority of rockhound collecting sites are on government lands managed by the USDA Forest Service or Bureau of Land Management (BLM). A few of these areas are designated as Wilderness Areas, meaning land use is strictly limited to entry by non-motorized vehicles, such as by foot or horseback. Areas so designated carry penalties for removal of any animal or plant species, as well as mineral or relic items. While surface collecting is allowed in Wilderness Areas, BLM collecting rules must be followed as to limits and methods. Generally, no more than a backpack full of material may be carried out using hand tools only.

Mechanical panning machines make cleaning up concentrates easy. PHOTO BY GARRET ROMAINE

The exception is petrified wood, which is limited to 25 pounds per day and no more than 250 pounds per year plus one large piece so as to avoid breaking a large specimen. Although large tracts of land have been set aside as Wilderness Areas, a great many collecting areas abound throughout the state, offering the rockhound a smorgasbord of sites to choose from.

Phone numbers for the primary BLM stations overseeing the southern California area are:

Needles: (760) 326-7000
Ridgecrest: (760) 384-5400
Barstow: (760) 252-6000
El Centro: (760) 337-4400
Palm Springs–South Coast: (760) 251-4800

Or go to www.BLM.gov/ca for more details and other California BLM ranger stations.

Note that there are many ongoing efforts to create new Wilderness Areas or closing areas entirely. Be sure to contact the appropriate BLM office for current status.

Because many collecting sites encompass wide areas, the GPS coordinates provided will not necessarily place you at the exact site, but will get you to the general location.

Earthquake Country

Earth's outer mantle, called the lithosphere, is about 60 miles thick. The lithosphere is broken into approximately twelve great plates that ride upon a partially molten layer of rock called the asthenosphere. The plates move and flow slowly in different directions upon the asthenosphere. Plates may slide past one another, pull away from one another, or collide, usually with one plate subducting below the other. Subduction of one plate below another usually results in volcanic activity along the overriding plate, as happens in the northern section of California extending upward into Alaska. Mount Lassen, in northern California, is the southernmost active volcano along this type of subduction zone.

Two of the approximately twelve great plates, the Pacific and North American plates, meet and grind past each other in California, creating the right-lateral fault known as the San Andreas.

The San Andreas Fault cuts through the southern portion and partway into the northern portion of the state. The Pacific and North American plates slip past each another at an average rate of about 2 inches per year, causing minor to moderate earthquake activity along various segments of its length from time to time.

During the great San Francisco earthquake of 1906, the Pacific Plate slid an impressive and monumentally destructive 20 feet in a northward direction past the North American Plate.

Frequent fault slippage along the San Andreas and hundreds of other smaller faults has made "California" synonymous with "earthquake." Yet it is only fair to note that California is just one of thirty-nine states in the Union known to have active earthquake faults.

Are earthquakes of major concern to mineral collectors and rockhounds visiting the state? Of course not (says this native Californian). Although California is famous for earthquakes, very few actually occur on a day-to-day basis, and most are of such low magnitude as to be unnoticeable. Besides, the safest place to be during earthquakes is away from the cities and in the countryside—say, for instance, on a rockhounding trip!

Sites to See

California's geologic diversity makes for a great variety of must-see locations that have little to do with actual, in-the-field rockhounding but everything to do with understanding and enjoying not only basic geology but also the unique geology of California.

Mitchell Caverns

Limestone caverns are a rarity in California. Why? Because limestone caverns are formed by two substances that California does not have in abundance, especially in southern California where the Mitchell Caverns are located. These two rare substances are water and the carbonates from which limestone is formed. The fact that Mitchell Caverns exist in southern California makes them unique.

Eons ago water percolated through the limestone of the Providence Mountains, dissolving cavities and tunnels and marking an ancient passage through the carbonate rock. The caverns lie in limestone wedged in by later intrusions of igneous rock and were formed millions of years ago when rainfall in the Mojave Desert was much greater than it is today. Over eons, dripping water has dissolved the limestone, creating fantastic and fanciful shapes and forming columns and forests of tubular stalactites, stalagmites, and flowstone.

Two separate caves, Tecopa and El Pakiva, joined by a man-made tunnel, form the Mitchell Caverns. The interiors of the caverns are easy to negotiate, since both have lighted walkways and stairs. Interesting features with names such as the Bottomless Pit and the Queen's Chamber intrigue visitors. Guided tours tell about the formation of the caves, as well as their history of habitation by both Native Americans and desert creatures.

Year-round temperature within the caves is 65 degrees Fahrenheit, so a sweater or light jacket may be in order for the tour. Park personnel conduct tours from mid-September to mid-June, as desert temperatures outside the caverns become unbearably hot in summer.

Self-guided tours include the nearby museum, which houses a host of mineral specimens collected from the local mountains, and a nature walk of about 0.5 mile. Signposts along the way inform and enlighten visitors about the local plant and animal life. For further information and tour times, call (619) 389-2281.

To get to Mitchell Caverns take I-40 east from Barstow, located at the junction of I-40 and I-15. Drive 102 miles to Essex Road. Turn left (northwest) and follow Essex Road for 9.7 miles to Black Hills Road. Take the left fork and continue 5.9 miles to the park's headquarters.

Death Valley

Death Valley has a magic all its own, and many have fallen under its spell. I know I have. As a result, I find myself making regular pilgrimages to imbibe the uncommon and severe beauty of its arid vistas.

The valley has a rich and colorful history of mining, tragedy, and misadventure. More than a century ago intrepid adventurers entered Death Valley looking for gold, and many remained in the valley after their mines were worked out. Most famous of the mines is the Harmony Borax Works. Today its ruins can still be seen by visitors. Worked from 1882 to 1889, a mere seven years, it became famous for its twenty-mule-team-drawn wagons.

Furnace Creek, Badwater, Salt Creek, Dante's View, Devil's Golf Course, and Hungry Bill's Ranch ruins are all interesting places to visit in Death Valley National Park. These names are also descriptive of the types of experiences pioneers and early travelers had when visiting or passing through Death Valley. The harsh conditions of blazing sun, little vegetation, scarce rain, devastating flash floods (when rain does occur), and wind erosion have created spectacular vistas that must be seen to be believed.

Death Valley is a place of extremes. Summer temperatures average 120 degrees Fahrenheit, with ground temperatures reaching 180 degrees, making Death Valley one of the hottest places on Earth. Fall, winter, and spring daytime temperatures average 60 to 70 degrees, although nighttime temperatures can fall to 40 degrees in winter. These cooler seasons are the time to visit Death Valley. In spring visitors may be treated to colorful wildflower displays, usually after a winter of some rainfall in the surrounding mountains. Very little rain actually falls in the valley. Most moisture enters the valley via flash floods that periodically roar down from the surrounding mountains.

Much of the valley's elevation lies below sea level. The lowest point accessible by car is Badwater, at 279.8 feet below sea level.

Other interesting places to see when visiting Death Valley include Scotty's Castle, a sprawling and richly appointed Spanish-Mediterranean-style mansion built by insurance millionaire Albert Johnson. Construction began in the 1920s, and the mansion eventually cost $2.5 million to build.

Johnson had a friend named Walter Scott, a generally unsuccessful but picturesque prospector whose flamboyance, tall tales, and eccentricity made him a popular character in his day. The irrepressible Mr. Scott, or Scotty to those who knew him, was a frequent guest at the Death Valley mansion. With his flair and talent for prevarication, he managed to convince many listeners that the mansion was his own abode, purchased with the profits from his fabulous gold mine. This fabulous gold mine existed only in Scotty's own

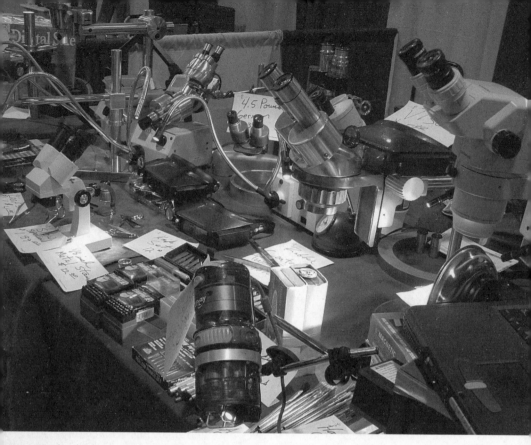

Vendor displays at rock and gem shows are a great place to view the latest in lapidary gear. PHOTO BY GARRET ROMAINE

vivid imagination, but he let slip subtle hints to avid listeners that it was located beneath "his" mansion.

Another interesting spot to visit in Death Valley is Ubehebe Crater, formed as the result of a violent volcanic explosion thousands of years ago. The crater is 500 feet deep and 0.5 mile across, and the landscape surrounding the crater is as barren and surreal as the surface of the moon.

The Racetrack is one of the most mysterious and intensely studied areas in the valley, by scientists and mystics alike. The 2.5-mile dry mudflat is the site of a little-understood phenomenon. Here rocks, both large and small, seemingly move unaided across the flats, leaving faint trails behind them. The courses left by the rocks can be straight or curved, or even seem to double back upon themselves. No one has ever seen the rocks move or captured the movement on film. Theories as to the cause range from extremely high winds to aliens!

While theories regarding the rocks' movements have been postulated, another curious phenomenon has gone unmentioned. Many wild burros inhabit the area and leave their organic excretions all over the Racetrack. This fecal detritus is also subject to the mysterious movement. However, the trails left by the burro droppings are often deeper and more apparent than those left by the heavier rocks. Here is a true mystery, one not as yet addressed—at least publicly—by the many experts who have studied the movement phenomenon. I visited this area some years ago with my partners, Mo and Ed Hemler, and we may one day return to Death Valley to attempt to solve this most unusual and, ummm, fertile mystery.

There are a variety of places to stay in Death Valley, including the plush inn at Furnace Creek, Furnace Creek Ranch, and Stovepipe Wells Village. RVers will find dry camping as well as full hookups available. Tent campers have at least nine sites throughout the park to set up camp and stay awhile.

Death Valley was designated a national park in 1995; therefore no mineral collecting is allowed within its borders. However, this guide lists several collecting sites outside Death Valley's boundaries. For your own safety, stay out of mines both within and outside the park.

Services in Death Valley are few and far between. When visiting, be sure to take extra drinking water. Frequently check your oil, fuel, and water temperature gauges. Keep tires at normal air pressure, as soft tires increase the chances of blowouts. If you have a breakdown, stay with your vehicle in the shade it provides. Park rangers patrol the paved roads on a regular basis. For more information call (619) 786-2331.

Natural History Museum of Los Angeles County

While there are many interesting and curious things to be seen at the museum, rockhounds will find the collections of dinosaur bones and fossils of particular interest. This museum also has an extensive mineral collection and one of the finest cut gemstone displays in the world. There is a fascinating collection of some of the fabulous gold nuggets found during California's gold rush eras. There are also hands-on displays for children. The Natural History Museum is located at 900 Exposition Blvd. in Los Angeles. For more information call (213) 744-3466.

George C. Page Museum of La Brea Discoveries

This museum is located just off CA 49 at the county fairgrounds near Mariposa in northern California. The mines near Mariposa were some of the richest in the mother lode. This museum displays more than 200,000 minerals, gems, and examples of mother lode gold. There is a hands-on mineral collection for kids, an assay office, and stamp mill models. What makes this museum unusual is an actual gold mine tunnel, which visitors can enter to see life-size depictions of mining scenes. Visitors can really get a taste of what gold mining was like at the turn of the twentieth century. This is the finest and largest museum in the mother lode country. For more information call (209) 742-7625.

California Wildlife

While seals, sea otters, and a large variety of seabirds are encountered on the coast, other types of wildlife are most commonly found in the mountain and desert regions. Both these areas are home to North America's largest feral cat, the cougar, and that wily trickster, brother coyote. Black bears and deer range throughout mountain regions; owls, rabbits, squirrels, and chipmunks are also frequently seen. Ospreys, condors, and eagles are less commonly observed.

Bighorn sheep roam some of the desert mountain areas but are elusive and rarely glimpsed. The only traces of their presence are usually cloven hoofprints in sandy desert washes, and these are often overlaid by the tracks of the desert cougar.

A wide variety of reptiles, from rattlesnakes, tortoises, and horny toads to chuckwalla lizards, inhabit the desert regions. Common to the deserts of California is the packrat, whose seed-packed middens can be found in nooks and crannies under rock overhangs. During twilight the engaging kangaroo rat may be seen hopping about on its long hind legs looking for a meal.

Deer, bobcats, and foxes also inhabit the deserts, their tracks evident around springs and natural seeps, which they visit during the early-morning and early-evening hours.

In springtime hairy tarantulas may be seen crossing dirt roads in the desert areas, while 1-inch-diameter holes covered with gauzy webbing mark the hideouts of trapdoor spiders.

Mourning doves, hawks, crows, and quail are common throughout the state, along with many varieties of songbirds.

Desert Travel

While a little common sense suffices for mountain traveling, desert travel requires some know-how and plenty of caution.

First in importance is your vehicle, which must be in good mechanical condition. Take extra belts and tools for minor repairs. Take plenty of water—several gallons for yourself and your group, as well as some for your vehicle should a radiator hose break. Take extra food in case of a breakdown. You could be waiting for several days before rescue arrives. During spring, fall, and winter, warm days often turn into freezing nights. Bring warm clothes just in case. I like to dress in layers so that I can dress up or down, depending on the conditions.

Tell someone where you are going and when you will return. Be specific, and stick to your schedule.

Stay out of old mines. Rotten supports, rattlesnakes, vertical shafts, cave-ins, and poisonous gases are just some of the dangers that await. The dangers far outweigh any imagined riches or relics you might hope to find. Remember, old mines have been abandoned because there is nothing more of value within.

The two reptiles to beware of are rattlesnakes and their deadlier cousin, the Mojave green, a rattlesnake mutation whose venom is a lethal neurotoxin. Look where you step, and be careful not to place your hands into crevices that you cannot see into. Rattlesnakes hibernate throughout the winter, emerging in March as the weather warms. However, not all rattlesnakes are aware of this schedule. They can emerge from hibernation early or late or even intermittently throughout the season, depending on weather conditions. Be cautious at all times.

California's Mineral Highlights

Gold

Gold is found throughout California, hence its nickname, "the Golden State." Although gold is found nearly everywhere in California, it is wise to keep in mind an old prospector's axiom: "Gold is where you find it, but it is not always found where you are looking!"

Serious gold prospecting requires skill, knowledge of geology and gold properties, and a few pieces of specialized equipment.

Gold panning, however, is an easy-to-learn activity in which many Californians indulge on weekends and vacations. They are often rewarded with grains and small nuggets. Panning for gold requires a gold pan, a small shovel, a pair of tweezers or tapered artist's paintbrush—for picking gold flakes out of the gold pan—and a small water-filled bottle in which to deposit the gold you find.

Basically gold panning consists of shaking and agitating water and gravel in the gold pan and gently sluicing off the contents until all that remains is the heavier black sand. The black sand is swirled aside, and if you're lucky you may see small gold flakes or even nuggets!

Especially when starting out, you'll benefit from hooking up with a local rock club.
PHOTO BY GARRET ROMAINE

As gold would be an attractive addition to any rockhound's mineral collection, I have included one gold prospecting site for southern California and one for northern California.

Fire Agate

Fire agate, different from regular agate, is actually a variety of microcrystalline quartz, or chalcedony. Fire agate forms in cracks, pockets, and fissures in rhyolite and basalt. Hydrothermal silica solutions seep into these crannies, where they cool and crystallize. Iron oxide in solution is laid down thinly between the layers of silica, creating multicolored fire. As additional layers of silica are deposited, botryoidal, or bubblelike, forms are created, which are typical of fire agate.

Vibrant iridescence, or "fire," is often seen through these lens-like bubbles of chalcedony. The darker the fire agate, the more likely it is to contain fire.

Mining and removal of fire agate is best done by hand. When I dug fire agate at Opal Hill Mine in early 1994, very careful pick and chisel work were essential to keep from breaking or cracking the fire agate, which is softer than the surrounding rhyolite. It is often necessary to remove an entire pocket of surrounding material to retrieve the fire agate intact.

Patience and careful grinding and polishing will further reveal and enhance the fire within. However, the fire layer is so thin that the lapidary must be careful not to grind through it. Another problem encountered when working with fire agate is that the fire layers are not flat but tend to pillow within the botryoidal bubbles. When working with fire agate, good lighting is recommended, as shadows deaden the fire and make it easy to overwork a piece. Frequently stopping to eyeball your piece helps ensure you are not polishing away the fire. Patience and care are the keys here.

Fire agate may be worked using flex shaft equipment or regular cabbing equipment. It is usually worked into baroque designs in order to enhance and follow the natural iridescence and color patterns of the stone. Some success can be had using a rock tumbler; however, it is possible to lose some of the fire with this method. A beautifully cut fire agate is a lovely and valuable gem that anyone would be proud to own, especially when you can say, "I found it!"

Benitoite

So far, benitoite has been found at only one location, the Gem Mine in San Benito County. Its composition is barium-titanium-silicate, and the color varies from near colorless to intense blue. The crystals form in triangular-shaped pyramids and prisms and are found in association with white natrolite and black neptunite in hydrothermal replacement deposits.

Due to its relative hardness of 6.0 to 6.5 and lovely blue coloration, benitoite is considered a gemstone. Due to its rarity, most people only see benitoite in jewelry stores and museums.

Tourmaline

Tourmaline occurs in almost every color. The famous watermelon tourmaline has a pink center surrounded by a "rind" of green. Tourmaline is a prized gemstone, whatever its color. Its crystals are columnar in shape and striated lengthwise.

Tourmaline occurs in granite pegmatites with microcline, lepidolite, and spodumene. One of the mineral treasures of California, it is found in the pegmatites of San Diego and Riverside Counties. Tourmaline is a rare and valuable gemstone, and most of the tourmaline-bearing pegmatites are held by private claim.

Black tourmaline, or schorl, is a more common variety that can be found by rockhounds hunting unclaimed pegmatite deposits along I-8 in southern California. Be sure that the pegmatites you are hunting are not claimed. Jewelry stores and museums are excellent places to view specimens of gem-grade tourmaline.

Common geodes. PHOTO BY GARRET ROMAINE

Legends and Lore of Gems and Minerals

Studying geology and collecting rocks, gems, and minerals are fascinating and satisfying endeavors in and of themselves. However, no study is really complete unless we know something of the traditional aspect of our subject in addition to our scientific examination. For rockhounds the study of geology often comprises both the historical and scientific features of our hobby. The personal history of rockhounding comes down to us in the form of the tradition and lore of the ancients.

To the ancients certain rocks, gems, and minerals had value not only as interesting collectibles or items of adornment but also, perhaps more importantly, as talismans, amulets, and medicines. Even today in Chinese and ayurvedic (Hindu) therapies, certain gems, minerals, and metals are used in infinitesimal amounts (often boiled with various herbs) for their supposed curative and restorative properties. Even the trusted family doctor may use gold in therapeutic injections for the relief of arthritis pain.

Traditionally stones were worn or carried as amulets or charms for protective or curative purposes, much as people today might wear a good-luck charm or religious medal. In ancient times a stone would often be inscribed with a magical symbol, glyph, or prayer to enhance the properties ascribed to it.

Many collectors are interested to learn of the traditional beliefs ascribed to minerals by ancient civilizations, tribal peoples, healers, and alchemists. Even today there are "New Age" beliefs concerning the curative powers of crystals and other stones, beliefs that have helped increase both the popularity and market value of many common stones—stones that rockhounds collect on a regular basis! Many retailers of minerals and gems have become knowledgeable in the lore of stones so that they may better serve their customers.

Ancient lore and traditional beliefs concerning gems and minerals enhance and augment rockhounds' studies and knowledge while also introducing an interesting historical facet to their hobby.

Rockhound's Vocabulary

Rockhounds use specialized terms to describe rocks, minerals, terrain, and other aspects of their hobby. Many of these terms are confusing to beginners and may not be found in your Webster's dictionary! Some terms are geologic jargon; others have evolved through the processes of invention and usage. I have included some of the more common rockhound terms here.

Cab or cabochon: A smooth-polished gemstone, usually but not always oval shaped and with a domed top. Generally it is cut, shaped, and polished but without facets.

Cast: A type of fossil. Not all fossils are shells or bones. Some are imprints left after the original substance has worn away, leaving an impression or cavity where the original lay. This depression is called the "mold." When silt, silica, or other substances fill the mold, a cast is created.

Chalcedony: A fine-grained, massive (rather than crystallized) variety of quartz. Its wide range of colors and patterns and varying degrees of translucence or opacity, as well as other elements in its makeup, have given rise to many different names in attempts to describe it.

Even rockhounds do not always agree on the names. "Agate" can be a catchall term and is sometimes used interchangeably with any or all of the terms used to describe types of chalcedony. Agate also describes a translucent

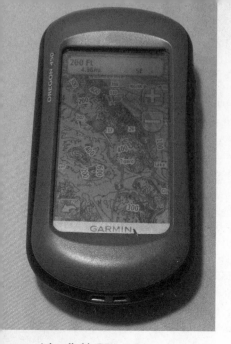

A handheld GPS unit is a great asset in the field. PHOTO BY GARRET ROMAINE

form of chalcedony with banding. Carnelian often refers to a translucent yellow, orange, or red variety, which may also have banding. Bloodstone, or heliotrope, describes a green variety with red spots, or any other color with red spots for that matter. Moss agate is a chalcedony that is white or clear, usually with dark, fernlike dendrites. Everyone pretty much agrees that chrysoprase is an apple-green variety, while jasper is opaque and solid in color, has a variety of colors, or has a variegated or mottled pattern. Flint is found in shades of white, tan, gray, or black, but then so are agate and jasper.

Many rockhounds have very firm theories concerning this issue and will contest opposing theories with great vigor. As stated, these rules are not cast in concrete nor agreed upon even by rockhounds. Even I, while fairly firm on some of the terms, still swap the terms jasper, chalcedony, and agate, as well as carnelian, sard, and sardonyx, with fairly free abandon. Hopefully this list, if it provides nothing else, will give novice rockhounds an idea of what they are in for when talking "agate" with old-timers.

Cleavage: The way minerals split along molecular planes, usually parallel to crystal faces, serving to identify many rocks and minerals.

Color: Often used as an identifying feature. However, color may be due to impurities within the sample and is not always a useful identifying property.

Country rock: The prevailing geology of an area that surrounds a vein or pocket of lode or gem material.

Crystal form (also called crystallography): Crystals form with a variety of faces based on their molecular structure. The placement, number, and shape of the crystal faces are identifying features.

Cutting material: Usually indicates rock or gem elements that are hard enough and dense enough for use in jewelry, sculpture, or other lapidary projects.

Dendrites: Fernlike inclusions in a mineral, usually of manganese or pyrolusite.

Desert varnish: A black or brown coating on desert rocks, usually as a result of iron or manganese oxides.

Druse or drusy: A crust of tiny quartz crystals.

Float: Material that has eroded away or fallen from a mineral deposit; often used by rockhounds to track a mineral back uphill to its source.

Fracture: The broken surface of a mineral. Noncrystalline rock forms often break along fracture lines rather than cleavage planes.

Portable radios are a great way to stay in contact when you explore a new area with a group. PHOTO BY GARRET ROMAINE

Hardness: One of several methods used to identify an unknown rock (see Mohs scale).

Igneous: Rocks or geologic formations that are a direct result or product of volcanism or deep-seated plutonics. Examples: basalt and granite.

Keeper: A slang term used to denote rock that is too good to throw away or leave behind.

Lapidary: The art of cutting or polishing stones or one who engages in the art.

Leaverite: Another slang term, which means the opposite of keeper. New rockhounds will often ask senior rockhounds what this term means. The neophyte will then be informed, "It's no good. So leave 'er right there!"

Luster: The way a mineral absorbs or reflects light, a useful identifying factor. Luster is classified usually as dull, earthy, silky, greasy, pearly, resinous, vitreous (glasslike), or adamantine (diamond-like).

Malpai: A flat area, devoid of vegetation; most often found in the desert. The area looks like man-made pavement, although it is natural. The "pavement" consists of desert-varnished rock and is often referred to as "desert pavement."

Metamorphic: Rocks that have been changed, usually by heat, pressure, or permeation. These changes often result in an alteration of the basic crystalline structure of the rock, as well as its appearance. Examples: gneiss, slate, marble.

Mohs scale: The relative hardness of rocks on a scale from 1 (softest) to 10 (hardest).

1. Talc
2. Gypsum
3. Calcite
4. Fluorite
5. Apatite
6. Orthoclase
7. Quartz
8. Topaz
9. Corundum
10. Diamond

This scale is useful when trying to identify an unknown rock or mineral. Some common materials display a hardness factor that can be used to help determine the identity of a rock specimen, even if one does not have all the minerals of the Mohs scale. A fingernail has a hardness of 2.5, a penny has a hardness of 3, a piece of glass or a knife blade has a hardness of 5.5, and steel has a hardness of 6.5. You can determine the hardness of a rock by scratching your unknown specimen on other rocks or substances of known hardness and then scratching these on your specimen. Harder rocks will scratch softer ones, while softer ones usually leave a powder trail on the harder rocks.

Sedimentary: Rocks formed by sediments of sand, silt, or mud that have become compacted and hard. Sedimentary rocks are often characterized by layering. Examples: sandstone, shale, conglomerates.

Streak: The true color a mineral makes when rubbed against a piece of unglazed porcelain. This is often different than the apparent color of a mineral and is a better identifying feature. This is particularly true of the metallic ores, where color and streak may be different because of impurities or oxidation.

Rockhound Rules

As mentioned above, I have been chastised for my "free-association" of terms regarding the various types of chalcedony. However, I have a theory: It is more important how one collects a rock than what one calls it.

So here is a brief listing of what I consider important rules for rockhounds of all ages, not necessarily in order of importance.

1. **Do not throw rocks.** This one applies to all ages for a variety of important reasons.
2. **Do not litter.** Following this rule is important if rockhounds want to continue to be welcomed at collecting sites. Marking areas with graffiti or defacing petroglyphs, pictographs, or intaglios are also considered vandalism.

Typical personal lapidary workshop. PHOTO BY SHEP KOSS

3. **Stay between the lines.** This means sticking to established roads and jeep trails. Driving off established routes not only defaces the landscape and destroys vegetation but also interferes with wildlife. In a desert environment especially, tire tracks take only moments to create but can remain for decades. If we are to maintain access to collecting areas, we must police ourselves. There are roads and jeep trails leading to our collecting areas; we do not have to stray from between the lines.

4. **Do not trespass.** Obey all No Trespassing, Do Not Enter, and Keep Out signs and those stating private mineral claims. This is not only a safety precaution but also respects the rights of property owners and claim holders. If you wish to collect on private property, always obtain permission first.

5. **Be prepared.** Be adequately prepared to administer first aid to yourself, your traveling companions, and your vehicle. Consider the weather, terrain, and other conditions you may encounter, and pack and plan accordingly.

Learn to use a hand lens and identify small crystals in the field. PHOTO BY GARRET ROMAINE

6. Do not be greedy. Pick up only what you can use or display, leaving specimens for others to collect—or yourself should you return to the site.

7. Leave animals alone. Gone are the days when you could take home a desert tortoise as a pet. They are an endangered species.

Rockhounding is an environmentally low-impact form of recreation, and most rockhounds act in environmentally responsible and respectful ways when out in the wilderness. So what are some of the things rockhounds are allowed to do when pursuing their hobby?

1. You may bend over, stoop, squat, crawl, or grovel in your efforts to find the perfect rock. In rockhounding no posture or position used to find a rock is considered too ignoble.

2. You may pick up a rock merely because you like it, whether anyone else approves. The selection of a rock or mineral is a highly personal matter.

3. You may dampen your rock to see its true colors and patterns. There are a variety of ways to do this. The extremely fastidious use a squirt bottle. The semi-fastidious (like me) lick them. And the old-timers spit on them.

4. You may take the kids. Not only are kids natural rockhounds, but they always seem to know where the really good rocks are hiding. Besides, there is nothing like the natural wonder of a child to reinstill a sense of wonder in adults.

5. You may take home only the best of what you find. Rocks take up lots of room. Before long your garage, yard, and home will be like mine, overflowing with them.

Rocks are beautiful. There are hundreds of things you can do or make with your rocks. They also look great just sitting on a shelf or windowsill. Visitors to my house always pick them up and admire them. Sometimes I give my rocks to guests who don't want to part with them. They make great gifts, and they are wonderful items to share with classmates during "show and tell." They are also good for trading and swapping for other good stuff.

Minerals found at tourmaline mines include lepidolite, green tourmaline, and schorl.
PHOTO BY SHEP KOSS

Rockhound Access to Commercial Mines

The famous tourmaline mines of the Pala District east of San Diego are mostly closed to the public. However, two mines regularly are open to the public as pay digs: the Oceanview Mine and the Himalaya Mine. The Oceanview requires online reservation through its website: www.digforgems.com. The Himalaya Mine website is www.highdesertgemsandminerals.com. To see or purchase lovely examples of tourmaline from these famous mines, visit The Collector, their museum/shop located at 912 South Live Oak Park Rd. in Fallbrook. Call (619) 728-9121 for more information.

One weekend a year, usually in October, the company that mines mineral-rich Searles Lake near Trona opens up certain sections to rockhound collecting. For current dates and other information, contact the Searles Lake Gem & Mineral Society (see listing in Appendix C).

U.S. Borax (now owned by Rio Tinto) no longer opens its mine to public collecting but instead regularly dumps collecting material in the visitor center parking lot. Check with the offices of U.S. Borax at Boron or Los Angeles for current dates, times, and restrictions, or call (760) 762-7588.

How to Use This Guide

This guide is divided into three sections: Rockhounding Sites in Southern California, Rockhounding Sites in Coastal California, and Rockhounding Sites in Northern California.

Maps are very important for finding collecting sites. Where possible, I have included information on other maps, such as US Geological Survey (USGS), USDAFS, or BLM maps, that cover the sites listed in this guide. These maps cover a wider area and show more details, such as geographical contours, buildings, springs, or other places that might be of interest to rockhounds.

When collecting in the desert, you will find many dirt roads that are not shown on any maps. New roads have been created by recreational off-road vehicles, making mileage and directional heading essential when attempting to choose between several dirt roads in order to get to your chosen collecting area.

In using maps to find locations, especially in the desert, it is helpful to have a directional compass along. Most compasses are affected by the electrical systems in automobiles and will not work properly inside a vehicle.

Automotive stores sell compasses that can be set to disregard the electrical systems of automobiles. They are generally reasonable in cost and well worth the time and small effort required to install.

USGS maps may be purchased at most sporting goods stores and cartography shops or ordered by writing or calling the Geological Survey division of the United States Department of the Interior and requesting their catalog. To get a copy of their catalog call (888) ASK-USGS (275-8747), give your address to the Science Information Specialist, and they will mail one directly to you. The waiting period for receiving ordered maps is up to a couple of weeks, so order in advance of your need for printed materials, or you can purchase and download them instantly via the USGS website, www.usgs.gov. Historic maps are available for purchase and download as well. The advantage to ordering maps directly from the USGS is that it is still possible to order some 15-minute maps, which are no longer printed and have become unavailable for purchase in most stores. They also cost less when ordered from their source. Most map shops sell only the 7.5-minute maps, and you must purchase several of these—each one costing the same as a single 15-minute map—in order to cover the same area depicted on a single 15-minute map. To make locating the sites listed in this book simpler, all references to USGS maps will refer to 7.5-minute series.

You may order BLM Desert Access Guides for southern California by calling (909) 697-5200. Maps are mailed immediately and will usually arrive two or three days later. The website, www.BLM.gov, will give listings of individual offices. Maps can be ordered through pertinent offices. USDAFS maps may be purchased at forest service ranger stations.

When possible, the GPS location of the site is listed; not all GPS information was available at the time of printing.

Mileage has been given with all site maps in this guide. Keep in mind that mileage may vary up to 0.2 mile from one vehicle to another.

Most collecting sites listed in this guide are located on public lands managed by the USDAFS or BLM. Most of the fee sites are located on land that is under valid mining or mineral claims or may be on patented claims. A patented claim is one where the government has deeded all rights and ownership of the land to the claimant.

When collecting rocks and minerals in California, it is important to be aware that land status is subject to change. Mining claims may be filed that overlay known collecting sites, and ongoing legislation may create new Wilderness Areas that encompass old collecting sites, making it illegal to remove anything from them. Be sure to obey all signs regarding current land status and respect all claim markers and No Trespassing signs. Above all be safe and have fun. Good rockhounding to you!

Map Legend

Symbol	Description	Symbol	Description
94	Interstate Highway	⋀	Campground
18	U.S. Highway	†	Cemetery
32	State Highway	▬	Dam
301	County Road	•–•	Gate
	Local Road		Lighthouse
= = = = =	Unpaved Road	Y	Mine/Tunnel
⊢–⊢–⊢–⊢	Railroad	▲	Mountain/Peak
•–•–•–•	Pole Line	◇	On/Off Ramp
– – – –	County Border		Overlook/Scenic View
– – ·· – –	State Border	P	Parking
Danger Zone		■	Point of Interest/Structure
Indian Reservation		✗	Rockhounding Site
Marine Corps Base/Military Reservation		35	Site Number
〜	River/Creek	⌒	Spring/Well
⬭	Body of Water		Tower
⬭	Wash	○	Town
⌣	Bridge	◪	Vertical Shaft

Fire Agate at Opal Hill Mine

Land type: Desert mountains
Elevation: 1,200 feet
GPS: N33 27.193' / W114 51.89'
Best season: November to April
Land manager: Private claim
Material: Fire agate, dog-tooth calcite crystals, gypsum, fluorite, quartz crystals, clinoptilolite
Tools: Sledgehammer, pick, chisels, gads, whiskbroom
Vehicle type: Four-wheel drive from Wileys Well; two-wheel drive from Palo Verde
Special attractions: Wileys Well, a watering station for the historic Bradshaw Stage Trail
For more information: Nancy Hill-Fisher, c/o Opal Hill Mine, PO Box 497, Palo Verde 92666
Accommodations: Camping available at Wileys Well and Coon Hollow Campgrounds and on the flats along the road from Palo Verde
Lore: Native American and Mexican lore holds that fire agate enhances tissue regeneration and energizes psychic centers.
Finding the site: To get to the mine, four-wheel-drive vehicles can exit I-10 at Wileys Well. Wileys Well Road is well graded and maintained by the BLM. However, only four-wheel-drive vehicles should attempt the 1.9-mile drive to the mine from Wileys Well Road. Two-wheel-drive vehicles should enter from the town of Palo Verde. Take the Fourth Street exit from CA 78 and follow the signs 9 miles to the mine.

Rockhounding

Opal Hill Mine is the only site in California where high-quality fire agate is found. Opal Hill fire agate is well known for its brilliant, cherry-red fire. However, iridescent greens (my favorite), yellows, oranges, and blues are commonly found as well. Of interest to micromount collectors, fine specimens of tiny quartz crystal clusters and crystalline flowers can also be found.

Amygdules containing crystals and nodules of fire agate have been unearthed. These are considered rare and very valuable if dug intact. As digging goes ever deeper into the mountain, a greater variety of minerals and collectibles continue to be disclosed.

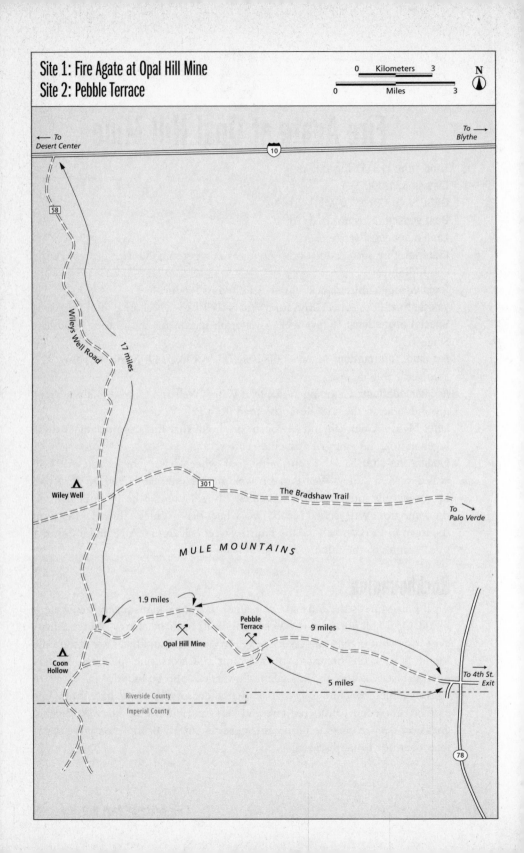

Site 1: Fire Agate at Opal Hill Mine
Site 2: Pebble Terrace

Kilometers   0   3
Miles   0   3

N

To Desert Center ←

To → Blythe

10

58

Wileys Well Road

17 miles

Wiley Well

301   The Bradshaw Trail

To → Palo Verde

MULE MOUNTAINS

1.9 miles

Opal Hill Mine

Pebble Terrace

9 miles

Coon Hollow

5 miles

Riverside County
Imperial County

To 4th St. Exit →

78

Fire agate from the Opal Hill Mine. Photo by Shep Koss

Many rockhounds may remember the mine's former owner, a cantankerous woman known for her prickly manner and salty language that was well peppered with expletives. She was also renowned in Palo Verde for driving her bulldozer into the town for a late-night binge at the local saloon. The mine has been under new management for more than eight years.

Nancy Hill-Fisher is the current owner and operator of the Opal Hill Mine. Her husband, Howard, assists in management. Nancy and Howard will help visitors locate and dig quality fire agate. Along with a three- or four-pound sledgehammer, rock pick, gad bar, and chisel, a whiskbroom is essential for sweeping aside dirt so that you can see when you've uncovered a nice piece of fire agate.

Specimens of fire agate also can be found by walking about with eyes glued to the ground. For those who prefer to acquire their fire agate with no exertion whatsoever, nicely finished and polished pieces are sold at the mine for very reasonable prices.

There is a daily per-person fee to dig at this site. Kids 12 and under dig for free. For those planning to spend several days digging, a few small trailers are available to overnight in. These overnight accommodations were available at no extra cost; however, this may be subject to change. Meals are not included, so bring your own food and beverages.

Pebble Terrace

(See map on page 26.)
Land type: Desert
Elevation: 980 feet
GPS: N33 27.372' / W114 49.561'
Best season: October to April
Land manager: BLM
Material: Multicolored moss agates, plume agates
Tools: Rock pick, collecting bag
Vehicle type: Any
Special attractions: Opal Hill Fire Agate Mine
Maps: USGS Thumb Peak
For more information: BLM Desert Access Guide Midway Well #21
Lore: Romans and Greeks used agate for protection and courage and believed that moss agate enhanced positive emotions.
Finding the site: From Palo Verde exit CA 78 at Fourth Street. Drive 5 miles to Pebble Terrace. You will see a sign that points the way to the Opal Hill Mine and informs you that you have reached Pebble Terrace. The sign also states that no commercial collecting is allowed. However, individuals and groups of rockhounds are welcome.

Rockhounding

This well-known site was favored by rockhounds from the 1930s well into the 1960s. Consequently the concern was that it might be overcollected, with little of interest to rockhounds remaining. This is not the case. The area still has abundant material; it's just hard to see! Desert varnish covers all the rounded agates, shaped by water. This area was underwater eons ago, and water action has left the area looking like the tide went out and never returned. This area is underappreciated today by rockhounds merely because it looks like nothing is here except a bunch of black cobbles of varying sizes.

The technique for hunting this area was shown to me by Herman Schob of Cathedral City. Pick up any rock and strike a glancing blow with your rock pick. This will dislodge a flake of the outer discolored skin and reveal the true color of the agate within. There are agates of bland and uninteresting color here, but there are also treasures hiding under the desert varnish.

Fossil impressions from Pebble Terrace. PHOTO BY SHEP KOSS

Hunting Pebble Terrace was like an Easter egg hunt. You never know what might be camouflaged at your feet. I found several beautifully colored and patterned agates. My prize was a palm-size cream-colored moss agate with green mosslike inclusions.

Black and Paisley Agate

Land type: Desert hills
Elevation: 820 feet
Best season: October to May
Land manager: BLM
Material: Black agate, lavender and green paisley agate, pink-and-cream-banded agate
Tools: Rock pick, bag, chisel
Vehicle type: High-clearance two-wheel drive recommended but not required
Special attractions: Thumb Peak and Clapp Spring
Maps: USGS Thumb Peak
Lore: Greeks and Romans wore agate for protection and to inspire courage.
Finding the site: From Wileys Well drive 5.6 miles south to an unmarked road to your left (east); park here, as this site is now in a designated Wilderness Area. To the left is the former road, now a foot trail. Follow this road 1.3 miles to a road on the left. Do not take this road. From this point continue 0.3 mile to the first site. There are seams of black agate on the low slopes to your left. Continue another 0.3 mile to the second site. On the slopes to your left is a location known for its lavender and green paisley agate.

Rockhounding

The black agate will require some pick and chisel work to remove. However, on one visit some kind soul had done the chisel work; all I had to do was pick it up and bag it. Some black agate, as float, will be covered with desert varnish. A glancing blow with your rock pick on the edge of the stone will chip off a section, revealing the color within. Most of the float is dull gray inside and of little interest to rockhounds.

The paisley agate was in short supply on my recent visit; however, I found fair amounts of a lovely pink-and-cream-banded agate reminiscent of wonderstone on the left slopes and also in the area to the right of the road.

The pink-and-cream agate made my visit well worthwhile. It would make beautiful cabochons for rings, small belt buckles, bolas, and brooches. Most pieces were palm size or smaller.

At first glance it may be difficult for rockhounds to identify the pink agate from the surrounding float, as it also is covered with desert varnish. A closer

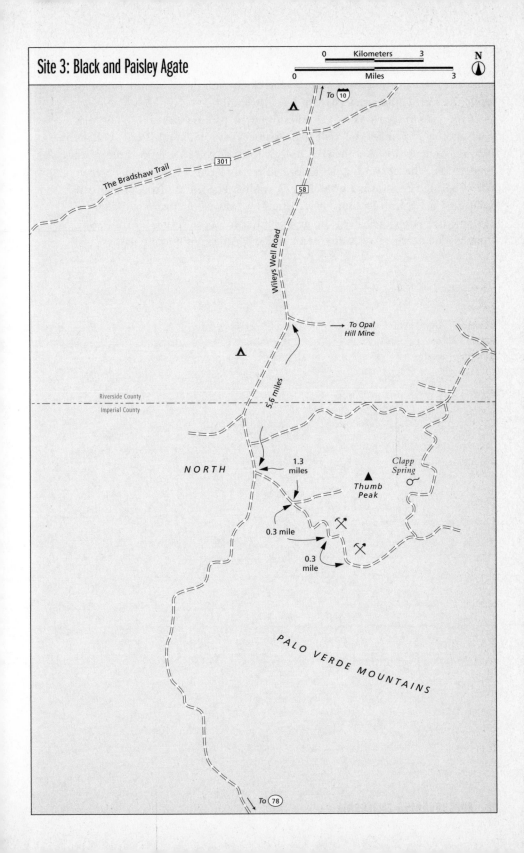

Site 3: Black and Paisley Agate

Kilometers 0 — 3

Miles 0 — 3

N

To (10)

The Bradshaw Trail — 301

58

Wileys Well Road

→ To Opal Hill Mine

5.6 miles

Riverside County
Imperial County

NORTH

1.3 miles

Clapp Spring

Thumb Peak

0.3 mile

0.3 mile

PALO VERDE MOUNTAINS

To (78)

look will reveal that the pink agate, even coated with desert varnish, is glossy, while the surrounding rocks have a dull matte finish.

If you take the left fork at 1.3 miles from the parking area and follow that road another 0.2 mile, you will have a fine view of Thumb Peak with its unique configuration. Another 0.2 mile will bring you to a fork in the road; veer left. For the next 3.1 miles ignore all roads to the left; you will arrive at Clapp Spring after crossing several sandy washes. The site is marked by several California fan palms. The spring was used by Native Americans and later by cattlemen to water their herds by piping water from the spring into watering troughs. The nearby caves were used by Native American hunting parties.

Crystal-Filled Amygdules

Land type: Desert
Elevation: 700 feet
Best season: October to May
Land manager: BLM
Material: Crystal- and zeolite-filled amygdule, chalcedony roses, calcite rhombs
Tools: Rock pick, bag
Vehicle type: Four-wheel drive
Special attractions: General Patton's World War II training field
Maps: USGS Little Chuckwalla Mountains and East of Aztec Mines
Lore: Greeks and Romans wore chalcedony to heighten peaceful, calm feelings and for protection while traveling or as a shield against negative energy. Europeans wore chalcedony for success in lawsuits and to increase lactation.
Finding the site: From I-10 heading west from Blythe, take the Ford Dry Lake exit onto Chuckwalla Valley Road. Head west for 2.8 miles to Graham Pass, marked with a vertical white post topped with an old whiskey bottle. From the east take I-10 and exit at Corn Springs onto Chuckwalla Valley Road. Head southeast for 13.2 miles to Graham Pass. Drive south on Graham Pass for a total of 9.1 miles (the road, as indicated on the map at 5.9 miles, is difficult to see from Graham Pass). At 9.1 miles turn left and drive 2 miles to the amygdule site. A four-wheel-drive vehicle may be needed to negotiate a twisting, turning drive through a large wash.

Rockhounding

The amygdule deposit is to the left of the road at the 2-mile mark and descends down into the wash. The amygdules are lima bean to fist size and contain a variety of crystals, mostly miniature, clear quartz crystals. More rare but worth looking for, some contain crystals of the zeolite group of minerals. These tiny quartz and zeolite crystals will delight the hearts of micromount collectors.

Most of the amygdules are loose in decomposed volcanic rock and are very plentiful. A few are still embedded, although easily removed with a rock pick.

Chalcedony roses also are found in the area. The roses are well formed, and whether merely cleaned up or tumble polished, they make lovely jewelry pins. They look especially elegant when set with a pearl or surrounding polished coral or black agate.

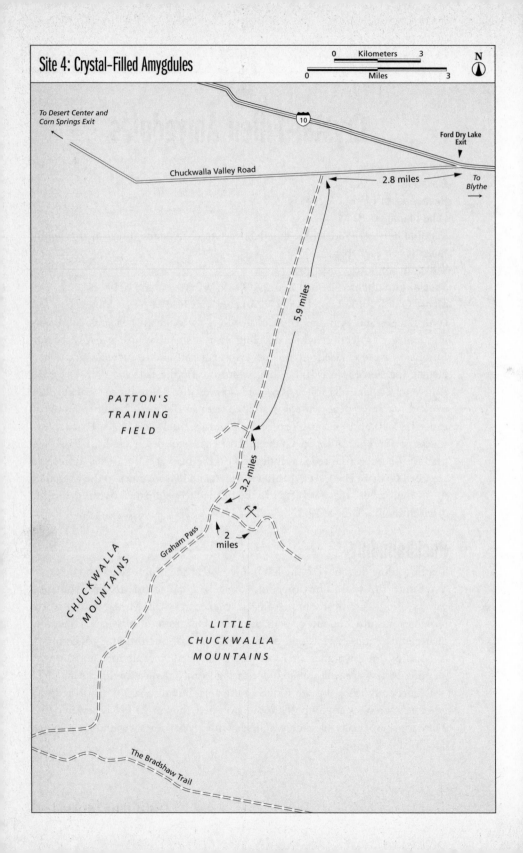

Site 4: Crystal-Filled Amygdules

Kilometers 0 — 3

Miles 0 — 3

N

To Desert Center and Corn Springs Exit

10

Ford Dry Lake Exit

Chuckwalla Valley Road

2.8 miles

To Blythe

5.9 miles

PATTON'S TRAINING FIELD

3.2 miles

2 miles

Graham Pass

CHUCKWALLA MOUNTAINS

LITTLE CHUCKWALLA MOUNTAINS

The Bradshaw Trail

Calcite rhombs are found by looking on the sides of the road. The calcite deposits are easy to spot; they look like circular patches of snow against the dark desert pavement. Some of the calcite is crystallized in the interesting rhombohedral form common to calcite.

Whether gently broken with a tap of the rock pick, sliced, or cut in half, the amygdules reveal their crystalline interiors and make interesting jewelry and specimen pieces. Tumble polishing smoothes and shines the chalcedony exterior of the amygdules. It reduces their thickness and reveals crystal points that shimmer and glitter beneath a thin skin of translucent chalcedony, catching the light in interesting ways.

At about 5 miles from the start of Graham Pass onward, on both sides of the road, is General Patton's World War II training field. Tank tracks may still be seen on the desert pavement. A friend of mine once found an old olive-drab flashlight and a sterling silver compass in this area. Interesting artifacts still can be found, especially in or near washes after heavy rains.

Hauser Geode Beds

Land type: Desert hills
Elevation: 1,150 feet
GPS: N33 22.567' / W114 59.383'
Best season: October to April
Land manager: BLM
Material: Agate- and crystal-filled geodes, red and green agate
Tools: Pick, shovel, rock bag
Vehicle type: Any
Special attractions: Historic Bradshaw Stage Trail
Maps: USGS Wileys Well
For more information: BLM Desert Access Guide Midway Well #21
Lore: In Europe geodes were believed to be the abode of elemental spirits and were related to female energy due to their egglike shape.
Finding the site: Because this is an extremely difficult site to find, I've provided chronological mileage.

From Wileys Well drive south on Wileys Well Road (M058) for 5.1 miles. Turn onto the road to your right. Set your mileage indicator to 0. Do not reset your indicator during the drive to the site. Drive 1.8 miles in a westerly direction. Veer right through a shallow wash and continue. At 4.3 miles take the left fork, which should be marked as M043. Come to another fork at 4.5 miles; stay left. At 5.3 miles take the fork to your right. At 6.3 you dip through a shallow wash. At 6.6 miles stay left, keeping to the well-marked road. At 6.7 miles take the road to your right. At 7.1 miles you come to a campfire ring near a large gully. Park here and walk down into and back up the other side of this gully. Continue walking.

When you come up out of the second gully, you'll find yourself on or near a narrow footpath to the left. Follow this footpath down through another gully. You'll lose the footpath where it rejoins the road through the gullies. As you walk, you will see a shallow wash to your left. Cross a shallow gully. Geodes have been dug all along this wash. Continue walking until a footpath heads directly to the wash at a shallow point. The walk is about 0.25 mile. Start digging where the ashy embankment is still intact at the far edge of the wash. The geodes will fall out as you dig.

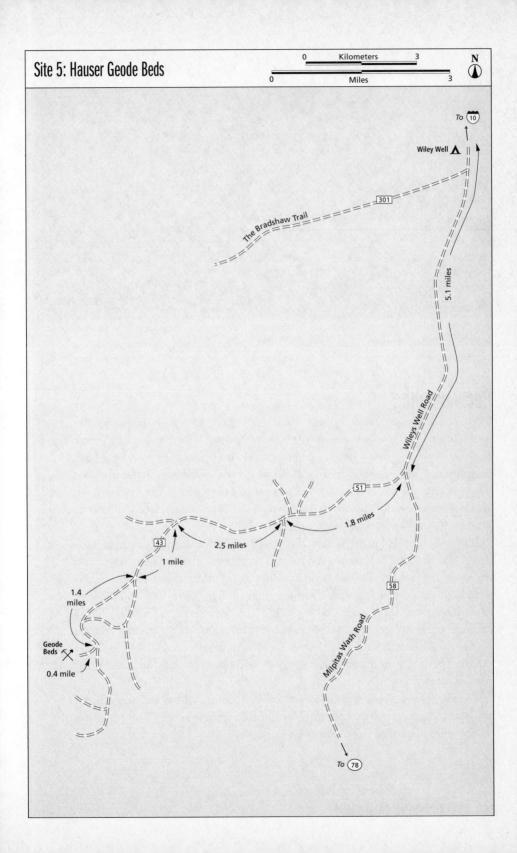

Kilometers

0   3

Miles

0   3

N

To 10

Wiley Well

The Bradshaw Trail   301

5.1 miles

Wileys Well Road

51

1.8 miles

2.5 miles

43

1 mile

1.4 miles

58

Geode Beds

0.4 mile

Milpitas Wash Road

To 78

Grapefruit-size Hauser Bed geode. PHOTO BY SHEP KOSS

Rockhounding

The Hauser Geode Beds are very difficult to find due to an interlacing of numerous roads. However, almost all roads in this area lead to numerous geode beds; unfortunately most have been completely dug out over the years. I have encountered many people driving about in this area looking for the beds but never finding the one they intended to visit or being sure if they had arrived at the one they wanted to search. The part of the Hauser Beds listed in this site is relatively unknown as of this writing.

The ashy embankment is soft and easily broken apart with a small pick or folding shovel. The best method is to scrape away the bank one layer at a time, picking out the fist-size geodes as they fall out. We uncovered many geodes in the shallow wash where you see signs of digging at the farthest point. Most have solid agate interiors displaying mottled markings in white, clear, beige, gray, chocolate, and a lovely pastel salmon. Some of the geodes contain a solid translucent agate interior with bands and streaks of white. One lovely double geode I found contained a cavity with perfect clear-quartz crystals massed inside.

On the narrow footpath leading out of the second gully, nice chunks of red and green agate can be picked up. Seams of this agate weather out from above on the mountains and roll down onto the path.

Psilomelane Near Wileys Well

Land type: Desert mountains
Elevation: 820 feet
GPS: N33 24.129' / W114 54.513'
Best season: October to April
Land manager: BLM
Material: Botryoidal psilomelane
Tools: Rock pick, collecting bag
Vehicle type: Any
Special attractions: Stone fortifications below psilomelane diggings
Maps: USGS Wileys Well
For more information: BLM Desert Guide Midway Well #21
Lore: New Age beliefs maintain that psilomelane, worn or carried, enhances psychic vision and development.
Finding the site: From Wileys Well drive south on Wileys Well Road (the name changes to Milpitas Wash Road at the Imperial County line) 5.5 miles to some low mountains to the right of the road. Pull off onto the flat area to your right. Walk up the side of the nearest low mountain to the signs of digging at the top.

Rockhounding

Though smaller in area than the Arlington Mine Site, this site is just off Wileys Well Road and easy to get to if you don't mind a little walk up the side of a low mountain. It is also convenient if you're visiting the other sites in the Wileys Well/Bradshaw Trail area. Good botryoidal and semimetallic cutting material is plentiful, as are nice velvety specimen pieces.

The stone fortifications, easily seen from Wileys Well Road, are interesting to see on your way up the mountain. A low stone wall has been erected along the flank of the mountain, and above that are several circular constructions. Opinions vary as to the purpose of these structures. Some speculate that they were built by prehistoric tribespeople as windbreaks. Possibly the structures were erected as fortifications during wartime training, although no ration cans or other recent debris is evident.

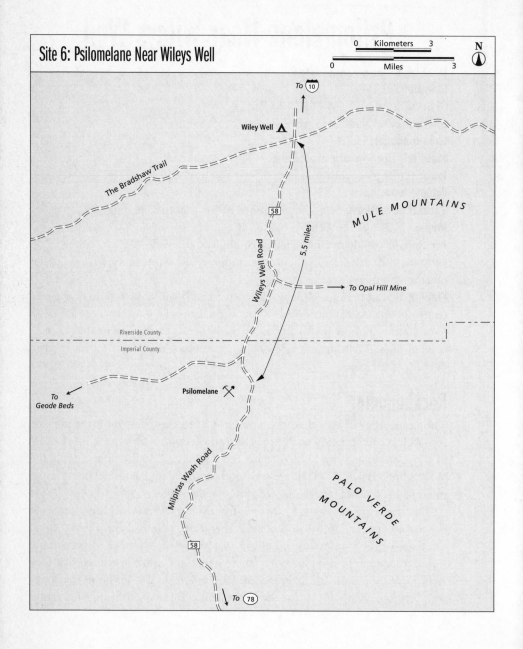

Site 6: Psilomelane Near Wileys Well

Kilometers

Miles

N

To 10

Wiley Well

The Bradshaw Trail

58

5.5 miles

MULE MOUNTAINS

Wileys Well Road

To Opal Hill Mine

Riverside County

Imperial County

To Geode Beds

Psilomelane

Milpitas Wash Road

58

PALO VERDE MOUNTAINS

To 78

Botryoidal psilomelane pieces. PHOTO BY SHEP KOSS

The desert varnish pebbles that litter the area between the mountain and the road are worth chipping with a rock pick to reveal their interior color. Some are lovely agates that would make colorful cabochons. However, be prepared to chip quite a few in order to find some keepers.

Chalcedony Rose Garden and Grossular Crystals at Augustine Pass

Land type: Desert hills
Elevation: 2,300 feet
Best season: October to April
Land manager: BLM
Material: Chalcedony roses, grossular crystals
Tools: Rock pick, collecting bag
Vehicle type: Four-wheel drive, dune buggy
Special attractions: Augustine Pass
Maps: USGS Augustine Pass and Chuckwalla Spring
For more information: BLM Desert Access Guide Salton Sea #20
Lore: Greeks and Romans believed that chalcedony, worn or carried, protected travelers and prevented nightmares. Early Egyptians and European alchemists held that clear grossular (a type of garnet) energized the pineal gland. It was also used to protect against crime, cure inflammation, aid the bloodstream, and strengthen the skeletal system.
Finding the site: From Wileys Well drive 0.2 mile south to the Bradshaw Trail. Turn right (southwest) on the Bradshaw Trail. *(Caution: Do not go south of the Bradshaw Trail. This area is a live aerial bombing range.)* Drive 27.3 miles and turn right onto a road marked with a rusted, hole-ridden water tank. At 1.4 miles bear right (east-northeast); continue 0.7 mile and park to the right at the foot of the hill. There is room here for several cars. The area is marked by a stone campfire ring. The mountain to the right is covered with chalcedony roses.

Rockhounding

To find the chalcedony roses, walk up and all around the mountain. The roses start out as oddly shaped, thin-skinned nodules. As you walk about the mountain, you will find the seams from which they erode. The nodules break as they weather out, which results in the classical lacy-shaped roses. Some are covered with white to buff drusy quartz that sparkles in the sun. All make nice jewelry pieces with cleaning and a little polishing of the edges. The roses may also be tumble polished.

If you drive another 0.5 mile over Augustine Pass, you will enter a deep, narrow wash. This is one of several rodingite contact zones where I was able

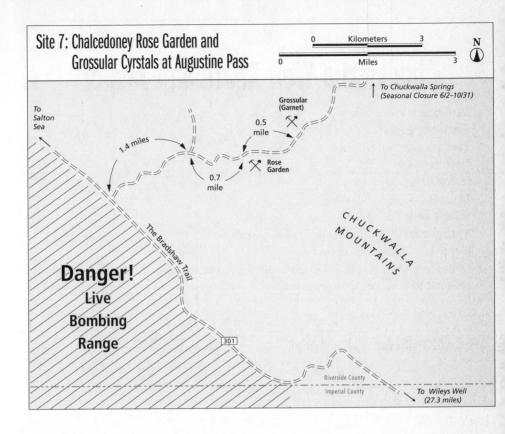

Site 7: Chalcedoney Rose Garden and Grossular Cyrstals at Augustine Pass

0 ___ Kilometers ___ 3

0 ___ Miles ___ 3

N

To Chuckwalla Springs
(Seasonal Closure 6/2–10/31)

To
Salton
Sea

Grossular
(Garnet)

0.5
mile

1.4 miles

0.7
mile

Rose
Garden

The Bradshaw Trail

Danger!

Live

Bombing

Range

301

CHUCKWALLA MOUNTAINS

Riverside County

Imperial County

To Wileys Well
(27.3 miles)

to remove nice pockets of grossular crystals using crack hammers, sledges, gads, and chisels. Most of the crystals recovered were crystal clear. Some were clear with chocolate matrices, and more rare was hessonite, which is orange-red in color. The rodingite contact zones show as green and red belts in otherwise grayish country rock.

On my last visit only a smattering of tiny crystals were visible on the rodingite contact at 0.5 mile. However, testing with a rock pick revealed several hollow-sounding areas that could be possible crystal pockets. Hard work is the only way to find out. Rodingite contacts occur in various places throughout the length of the pass.

Augustine Pass has been the site of considerable mining, most likely for gold, from the late 1800s through 1930. Mining relics can be found throughout the pass. In 1905 a bleached skeleton was found at the pass, a rusted gold pan and a pocket watch nearby. Only short-base four-wheel-drive vehicles are recommended for driving through the pass to Chuckwalla Springs. This seasonal route is closed from June 2 through October 31.

Chuckwalla Well Agate and Jasper

Land type: Desert hills
Elevation: 2,100 feet
Best season: November to April
Land manager: BLM
Material: Agate, jasper
Tools: Rock pick, collecting bag
Vehicle type: Four-wheel drive
Special attractions: Bradshaw Trail explorations
Maps: USGS Chuckwalla Spring
Lore: The ancients wore agate and jasper for protection and courage. Jasper was believed to have rain-bringing qualities.

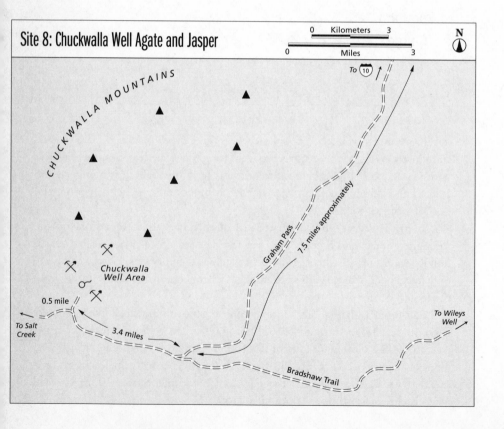

Site 8: Chuckwalla Well Agate and Jasper

Finding the site: From Chuckwalla Valley Road take Graham Pass Road approximately 17 miles south to the Bradshaw Trail. Head west (right) on the Bradshaw Trail for 3.4 miles. Turn right onto a road and drive an additional 0.5 mile. Search the hills that rise up behind the well area.

Rockhounding

Agate in a variety of colors and patterns may be found upon the hills and all along their bases. Jasper in orange-red, yellow, maroon, and green can be found here too.

The well is a gathering place and watering hole for many desert animals. Try to park away from the well so as not to disturb their comings and goings. The best collecting is away from the well and along the hillsides behind it.

Psilomelane at Arlington Mine

Land type: Desert mountains
Elevation: 1,100 feet
Best season: Late September to May
Land Manager: BLM
Material: Botryoidal psilomelane
Tools: Rock pick, collecting bag
Vehicle type: Any
Special attractions: Giant Indian intaglios (desert drawings)
Maps: USGS Arlington Mine and Inca
For more information: BLM Parker/Blythe Desert Access Guide #16
Lore: New Age believers maintain that psilomelane, worn or carried, enhances psychic vision and development.
Finding the site: To reach the Arlington Mine, exit I-10 at Lovekin Road and head north (as the road heads northwest it becomes Midland Road). Drive Lovekin/Midland Road for 18 miles to a huge white boulder of gypsum to your left. Turn left here and head west. At 1.6 miles cross a railroad track and enter what remains of the small burg of Inca. Just past the tracks, another 0.1 mile, take the right fork and continue west for 9 miles on P172 (at one time a fully paved road).

Small piles of a white substance litter both sides of the road. This is gypsum from the U.S. Gypsum Mine, 3 miles to the north on a slope of the Little Maria Mountains. At the 9-mile mark take a road to your left heading to some diggings on the flank of a broad, low mountain. The road leads straight to the diggings. You may park or continue on to several higher levels. Psilomelane, one of the principle ores of manganese, litters the ground and is piled up everywhere.

Rockhounding

The Arlington Mine actually comprises several claims and diggings that were active during World Wars I and II. However, the first and largest site is usually referred to as the Arlington Mine. Manganese, a major component of psilomelane, is used to harden steel and in the manufacture of armaments. The mine is currently inactive. Look for velvety black botryoidal masses or semi-metallic pieces as specimens or cutting material.

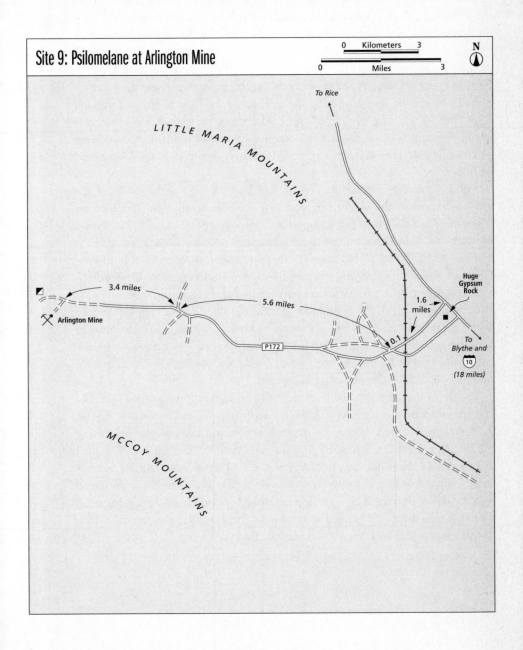

Site 9: Psilomelane at Arlington Mine

Kilometers 0 3

Miles 0 3

N

To Rice

LITTLE MARIA MOUNTAINS

3.4 miles

5.6 miles

Arlington Mine

P172

Huge Gypsum Rock

1.6 miles

0.1

To Blythe and 10 (18 miles)

MCCOY MOUNTAINS

If you cut across the botryoidal mass, shaping and polishing will result in a gemstone with the silvery look and luster of hematite but displaying concentric charcoal-colored rings. Psilomelane is slightly softer than hematite, 5 on the Mohs scale, but makes a beautiful gem as well as an interesting addition to a mineral collection.

Also at the Arlington Mine, thin mantles of drusy quartz and chalcedony form in layers within contact zones between the psilomelane and the country rock. These can be found littering the ground or attached to the psilomelane fragments. In the case of the Arlington Mine site, the best psilomelane collecting seemed to be on the lower levels in and around the parking area. Easy pickings! Just drive to the site, step out, stoop over, and pick it up. What could be better?

Psilomelane diggings farther out on P172 are visible on the flanks of the low mountains to the left of the road. Just previous to my visit to the mine heavy rains and flash flooding had partially destroyed portions of P172 beyond the first site. Although I visited these other digs, a 4x4 was required. P172 is maintained by the BLM and may have been repaired since my visit, but heavy rains and subsequent flooding often re-damage or undo recent repairs made to roads. Check with the BLM for current conditions before your visit.

Although much of the diggings in the Arlington Mine area appear to have been strip-mined, there is the occasional tunnel and shaft, so be cautious in your explorations. Although I saw no other vehicles on P172 during my visit, large mining vehicles use the road when the U.S. Gypsum Mine is active. Be ready to yield the right-of-way if necessary.

To get to the larger-than-life giant Indian intaglios (pronounced *in-TAL-yos*) return to Blythe and take CA 95 approximately 12 miles north of Blythe. To the right will be a large stone monument with a brass plaque describing the intaglios. Turn left across the highway and proceed east on a well-graded dirt road for a short distance, until you see several fenced areas to the right. A short and easy walk will bring you to the intaglios. The intaglios were traced into the desert pavement by ancient peoples and are protected by fencing from trespass. Their shapes are easily discerned from the ground and spectacular from the air, should you have the opportunity to fly over them.

Orocopia Bloodstone

Land type: Desert hills
Elevation: 1,400 feet
Best season: November to April
Land manager: BLM
Material: Bloodstone, red and green jasper
Tools: Collecting bag, rock pick, crack hammer
Vehicle type: Four-wheel drive
Special attractions: Historic Bradshaw Trail area
Maps: USGS Hayfield
For more information: BLM Desert Access Guide Chuckwalla #18
Lore: Legend states that green jasper was placed at the foot of the cross and was flecked with blood from Christ's wounds, thereby becoming bloodstone. Worn, bloodstone draws wealth, predicts weather, aids in legal battles, eases labor pains, and increases crop yield; it stanches bleeding when held to a wound. Popular during biblical times, it was called heliotrope.
Finding the site: Exit I-10 at Red Cloud Road. Drive 13.8 miles along the Mining Railroad. Part of the drive is through a wide, sandy wash. Turn right into a canyon and drive a few hundred yards to a BLM sign that tells you not to drive any farther. From here walk a couple hundred yards northwest to where two washes converge. On the slope between the two washes you will find abundant bloodstone.

Rockhounding

The site is abundant in red and green jasper in many patterns, much with red flecks. Also found is green jasper with translucent white agate and dark green jasper with bold jagged lines, much like lightning bolts.

This area is completely closed from June 1 to November 1, so plan your visit accordingly. The temperatures November through April are more comfortable.

This area has a small spring that seeps year-round, making it an essential watering place for desert wildlife when other springs in the area dry up during the hot summer.

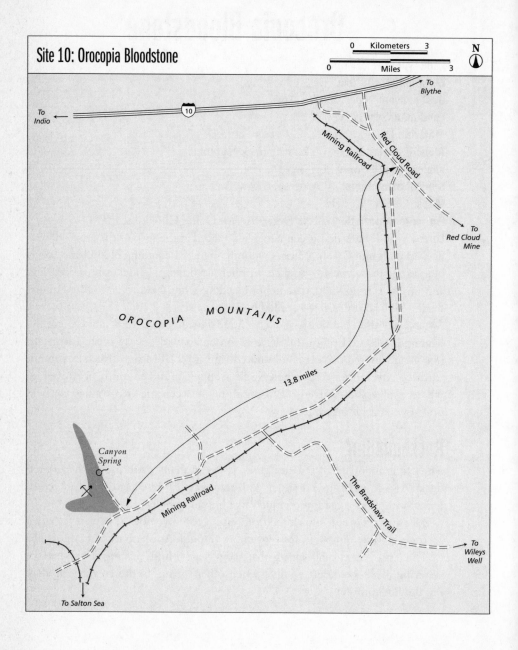

Site 10: Orocopia Bloodstone

Kilometers

0   3

0   Miles   3

N

To Blythe

To Indio

10

Mining Railroad

Red Cloud Road

To Red Cloud Mine

OROCOPIA MOUNTAINS

13.8 miles

Canyon Spring

Mining Railroad

The Bradshaw Trail

To Wileys Well

To Salton Sea

Orocopia Fluorspar

Land type: Desert hills
Elevation: 2,400 feet
GPS: N33 37.26' / W115 41.13'
Best season: October to April
Land manager: BLM
Material: Fluorspar
Tools: Rock pick, collecting bag
Vehicle type: Four-wheel drive
Special attractions: None
Maps: USGS Orocopia Canyon
Lore: In New Age lore fluorite assists mental function and allays mental fatigue. It is useful to keep near computers, as it is reputed to enhance their function and prevent breakdowns.
Finding the site: Exit I-10 at Chiriaco Summit. Just south of the freeway, take the road heading west 1.3 miles to a dirt road on your left. Take this dirt road (SR 2013) south 1.8 miles to a fork. Take the left branch southeast 1.4 miles to another fork. Again bear left and continue 1.8 miles. Turn right off SR 2013 onto a rocky, poorly maintained road heading up the hill. Drive 0.2 mile—a bit farther if you can—until the road heads sharply uphill. Park at the base of this incline. On foot follow a narrow wash that is about 3 feet deep and lies to the right of the road. Walk this wash about 50 feet, then hike a short way up to the top of the hill on your right. Here you will find a shallow pit with vast quantities of fluorspar.

Rockhounding

This is the site of a long-abandoned fluorspar mine. Fluorspar, a variety of fluorite that crystallizes in needlelike crystals rather than the more common cubic variety, is used in steel and ceramic making.

Although a little on the soft side, fluorite makes lovely jewelry and cabochons. When sawed into slabs, the fluorspar from this site is suitable for lapidary projects. It is translucent to clear in cream, yellow, green, brown, and violet. My favorite is the cream with violet banding. The material from this location also makes nice tumbled pieces for the kids' jewelry projects. It will fluoresce under an ultraviolet lamp.

Site 11: Orocopia Fluorspar

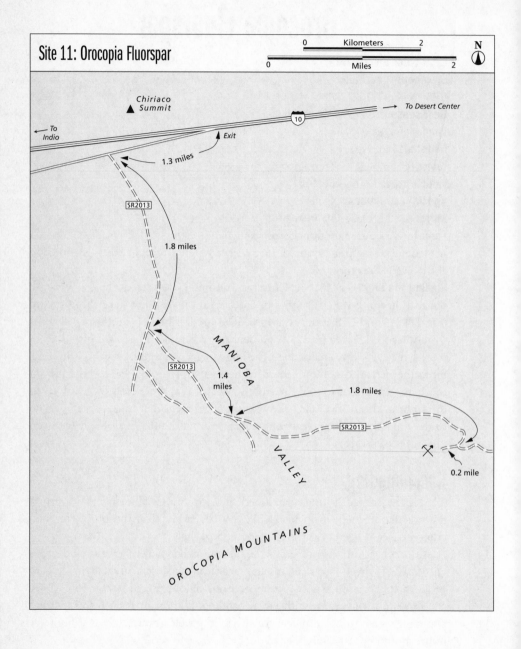

Big River Botryoidal Chalcedony with Drusy Quartz, Jasper, and Agate

Land type: Desert
Elevation: 1,180 feet
GPS: N34 10.88' / W114 22.58'
Best season: October to April
Land manager: BLM
Material: Botryoidal chalcedony with drusy quartz, jasper, and agate
Tools: Rock bag, pick
Vehicle type: Any
Special attractions: Colorado River camping and recreation
Maps: USGS Parker and Parker NW
For more information: BLM Parker/Blythe Access Guide #16
Lore: Chalcedony and drusy quartz offer protection during travel and freedom from nightmares. Jasper is the rain bringer and healer of bodily ills.
Finding the site: From CA 62, as you're heading east, proceed 2.3 miles past Rio Mesa Road and turn left (north) onto a dirt road with a sign reading PRIVATE ACCESS ROAD. This road is maintained by the water district and goes to the Colorado River Aqueduct. You are permitted to travel on this road to get to the collecting site. Drive north 4 miles; turn right just past the beehives, heading 0.2 mile to the base of a hill. The area west of the hill has been graded. Nice specimens of botryoidal chalcedony in both cream and pink, with a sparkling coating of drusy quartz crystals, will be found in varying sizes.

To reach another nearby collecting location with jasper and agate, head 0.3 mile west past Rio Mesa Road. Turn right and head north for 1.4 miles. (Ignore the road heading in a westerly direction at 0.6 mile.) This site yields red jasper and a variety of pink and white agate.

Rockhounding

The first site at 2.3 miles east of Rio Mesa Road is reputed to have excellent red, yellow, and rainbow jasper among an abundance of very poor, grainy material. Perhaps this was true many years ago. On my visit, although I searched the area, I found only very poor quality jasper. The area may be more productive after a heavy rain just north of the foot of the mountain. At present there is

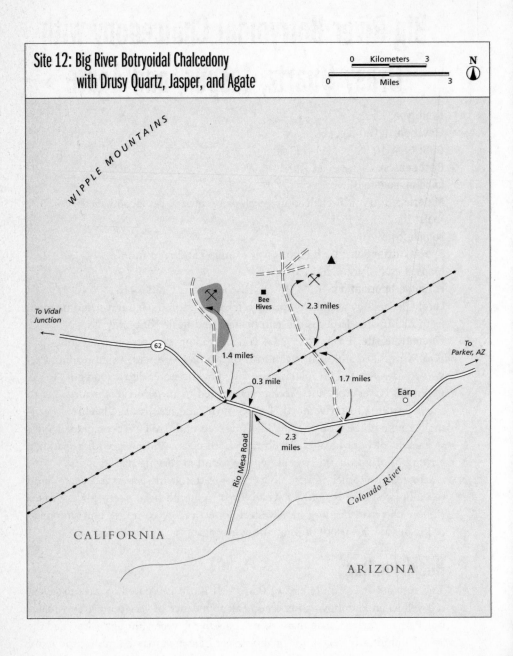

Site 12: Big River Botryoidal Chalcedony with Drusy Quartz, Jasper, and Agate

0 Kilometers 3

0 Miles 3

N

WIPPLE MOUNTAINS

To Vidal Junction

62

1.4 miles

Bee Hives

2.3 miles

0.3 mile

1.7 miles

Earp

To Parker, AZ

Rio Mesa Road

2.3 miles

Colorado River

CALIFORNIA

ARIZONA

a chain across the opening of the wash, so you will not be able to drive into it. The only item of interest in this area is the sparkling, drusy-quartz-covered chalcedony in both pink and cream. This material will make nice baroque pins, pendants, and bolas if the edges are ground and smoothed and a silver or gold bezel is added.

The second location, 0.3 mile west of Rio Mesa Road, is the more productive of the two as far as agate and jasper are concerned. To the east of the road about 50 feet is a shallow wash. I had my best luck collecting along the length of this wash, where I found mottled pink-and-cream as well as red-and-cream agate, along with a few pieces of red jasper. There also were some scattered pieces of white chalcedony with gray banding. Some walking and looking is required, as the material is not abundant. After twenty minutes of walking about, you may find a nice collection of cutting material. This is not a trip to take in and of itself. However, if you are vacationing in the Colorado River area, this trip makes a nice break from nearby water recreation.

If you are planning a trip to this area during the first two weeks of April, bring your camera to photograph the beautiful, vibrantly pink and fuchsia blooms of the beavertail cacti that line the road leading to the more productive of the two locations.

Turtle Mountains
Snowy Chalcedony Roses

Land type: Desert
Elevation: 1,312 feet
Best season: October to April
Land manager: BLM
Material: Snowy white desert roses
Tools: Rock pick, collecting bag
Vehicle type: Any
Special attractions: Turtle Mountains
Maps: USGS Stepladder Mountains and Snaggletooth

Desert palms are part of the varied flora in the California deserts.
PHOTO BY GARRET ROMAINE

Site 13: Turtle Mountains Snowy Chalcedony Roses

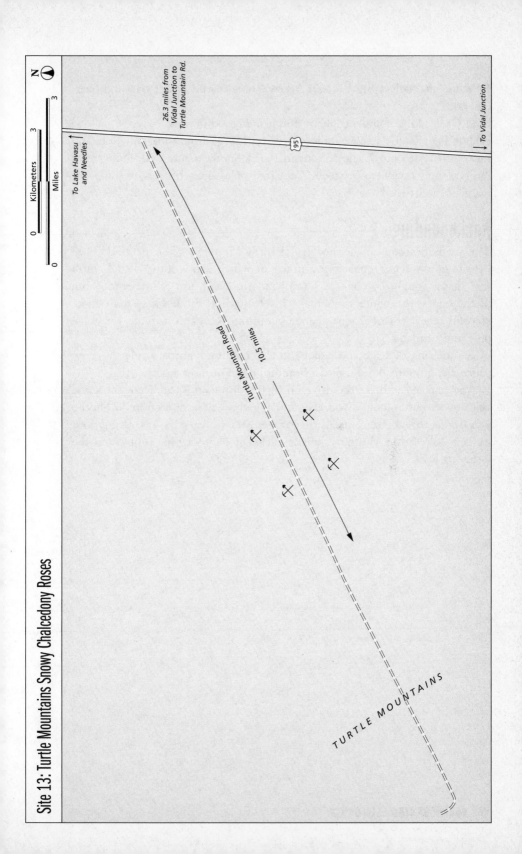

N

Kilometers

Miles

To Lake Havasu and Needles

95

To Vidal Junction

26.3 miles from Vidal Junction to Turtle Mountain Rd.

Turtle Mountain Road

10.5 miles

TURTLE MOUNTAINS

For more information: BLM Desert Access Guide Blythe/Parker #16 and Needles #13

Lore: Chalcedony represents purity and brings good dreams.

Finding the site: Drive 26.3 miles north on US 95 from Vidal Junction, and turn left (west) onto Turtle Mountain Road. Snowy white chalcedony roses can be found anywhere between 9 and 10.5 miles along the side of this well-maintained dirt road.

Rockhounding

This site is located near the spectacular Turtle Mountains. The material found here is snowy white chalcedony, much of which forms into the delightful rose shapes sought by collectors and lapidaries. With just a little smoothing of the edges, the white roses make lovely settings for black pearls or any colorful spherical or baroque-shaped gemstone. Roses are naturals for bolas, pins, and pendants.

A scattering of agate and jasper can also be found, but as a rule these are scarce along the road. I did find a beautiful piece of moss agate.

Any vehicle can make the drive on Turtle Mountain Road. There are some sandy spots, but as long as you keep moving you will have no trouble. Should you decide to explore some of the washes, you will need a 4x4. Bring your camera—the Turtle Mountains make excellent photographic subjects in the changing light.

Lake Havasu Agate

Land type: Desert
Elevation: 918 feet
Best season: October to April
Land manager: BLM
Material: Colorful agate
Tools: Rock pick, collecting bag
Vehicle type: Four-wheel drive
Special attractions: Lake Havasu
For more information: BLM Desert Access Guide Parker/Blythe #16
Lore: Agate is used for courage, strength, and protection.
Finding the site: From US 95 north of Vidal Junction turn right (east) onto Lake Havasu Road. Continue east for 10 miles to where the power lines cross the road. Drive 2 more miles to a dirt road to your right. Shortly after you turn onto this dirt road you will see a large rock monument that reads HAVASU MINING AND MINERALS. Drive 1 mile to the hill, which is marked with streaks of light-colored ash. The entire hill is made of agate and jasper in many patterns and colors.

Rockhounding

This is a great place to collect agate and jasper. The entire hill rising from the wash is composed of colorful agate and jasper in a variety of hues and patterns. The road is firm, and any vehicle can make it except for the last 0.2 to 0.3 mile. The agate and jasper hill is located in a large wash, which will make a 4x4 necessary if you don't want to walk that last bit.

The collecting material comes in fist to boulder sizes. There is plenty to pick up. The highly energetic may wish to bring chisels, sledges, and gads to remove agate in situ, but there is so much just laying about that it is not really necessary.

Somewhere on the side of the hill near the second seam of white ash is a small deposit of chrysocolla. Although I was unable to find the deposit, I found numerous small pieces of chrysocolla float near the base of the ash seam.

Lake Havasu Recreation Area is on the Chemehuevi Indian Reservation. A permit is required to visit or camp at the lake. Permits can be obtained at a gate prior to entering the recreation area.

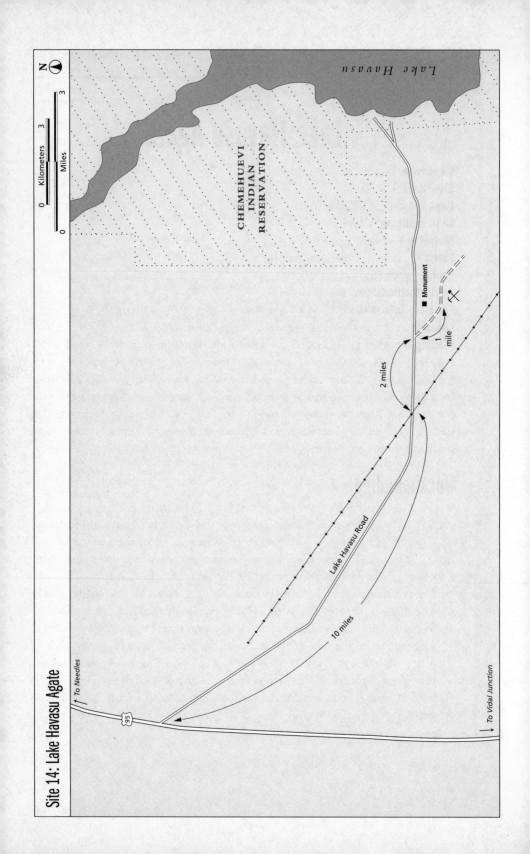

Site 14: Lake Havasu Agate

Dendritic White Opalite at Goffs

Land type: Desert hills
Elevation: 3,200 feet
Best season: October to April
Land manager: BLM
Material: Dendritic white opalite, agate, jasper
Tools: Rock pick, collecting bag
Vehicle type: Any
Special attractions: None

Some roads just aren't meant to be traveled by minivans and sedans.
PHOTO BY GARRET ROMAINE

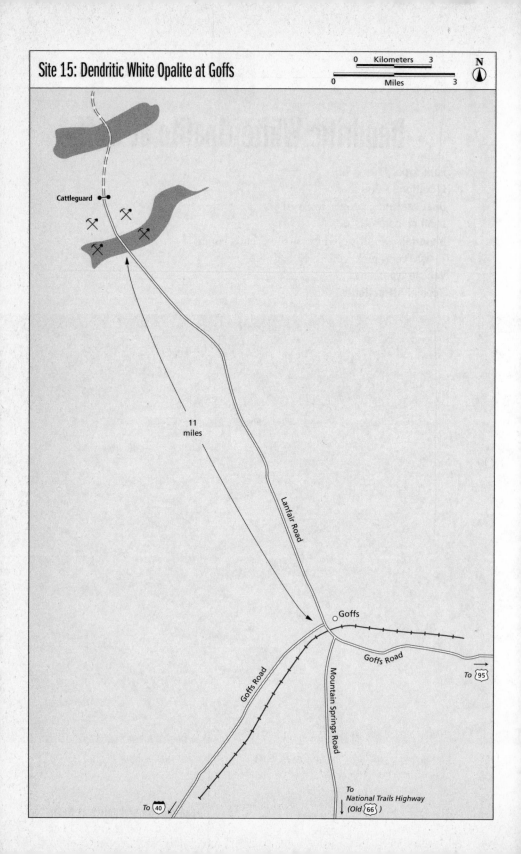

Site 15: Dendritic White Opalite at Goffs

0   Kilometers   3

0   Miles   3

N

Cattleguard

11 miles

Lanfair Road

Goffs

Goffs Road

Goffs Road

Mountain Springs Road

To 95

To 40

To
National Trails Highway
(Old 66)

Maps: USGS Goffs

For more information: BLM Desert Access Guide New York Mountains #9

Lore: Opalite balances left and right brain hemispheres and lightly stimulates the glands.

Finding the site: You may access Goffs Road from either I-40 or US 95. From Goffs Road, near the tiny town of Goffs, turn onto Lanfair Road and head north 11 miles. Park along the road where the wash crosses it. Slightly farther on you will cross a cattleguard and come to a second, less-productive wash.

Rockhounding

This site is located in free-range cattle country, so exercise caution when driving on Lanfair Road. When you exit your car at the collecting site, you may see cattle about. Not being familiar with bovine protocol, I adopted the policy of ignoring them. It must have been the right thing to do, because they ignored me as well. Mind you, these happened to be all cows with calves. The ignoring policy may not work with bulls, so use caution when collecting near cattle.

Nice palm-size pieces of white opalite with black dendrites are found in the wash, particularly on the east side of the road where the wash enters a rocky canyon. (The cows also favor this side of the wash.) White opalite with translucent, amber-colored agate centers can occasionally be found, as well as some red jasper.

Danby Opalite and Agate

Land type: Desert hills
Elevation: 1,300 feet
Best season: October to April
Land manager: BLM
Material: Colorful opalite and agate
Tools: Collecting bag, rock pick, shovel
Vehicle type: Any
Special attractions: None
Maps: USGS Danby, Skeleton Pass, and Cadiz Summit
For more information: BLM Desert Access Guide Sheephole Mountains #12
Lore: Opalite is mildly stimulating to the glandular system. Agate encourages strength, courage, and protection.
Finding the site: From the National Trails Highway (Old US 66) take Danby Road southeast for 1.7 miles. After crossing the railroad tracks, turn right and follow the road that runs parallel to the railroad tracks for 6.8 miles. Turn left onto a dirt road and travel 0.5 mile. I have marked this road with two rock cairns on the left. This dirt road can be traversed by any vehicle; other dirt roads in the area require a 4x4.

Rockhounding

The opalite and agate are most abundant on the left side of the road at 0.5 mile. Plenty of small sizes, ready for the tumbler, can be found here. There are some larger pieces found aboveground as well. Use your shovel to dig into the soft, fine sand for larger pieces.

The material comes in a variety of colors and patterns. The agate here is particularly beautiful in translucent red and orange shades. Most of the opalite occurs in rose pink and white.

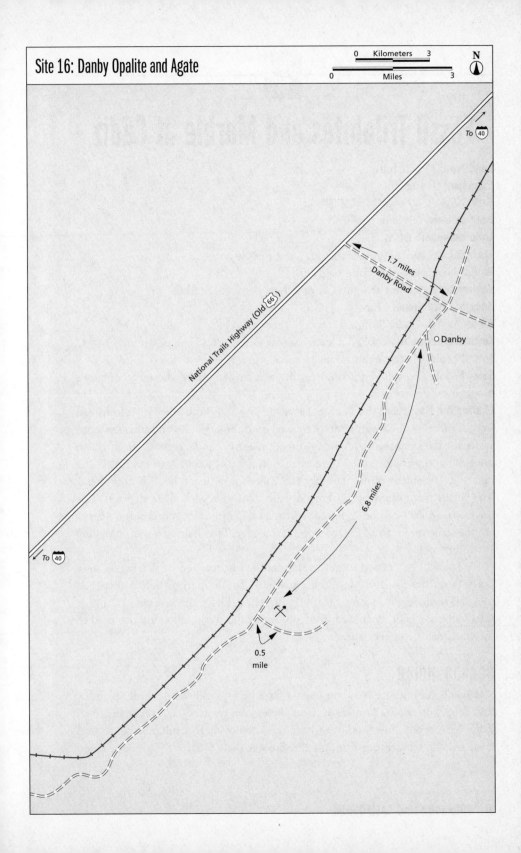

Site 16: Danby Opalite and Agate

Fossil Trilobites and Marble at Cadiz

Land type: Desert hills
Elevation: 918 feet
GPS: N34 32.17' / W115 28.57'
Best season: October to April
Land manager: BLM
Material: Fossil trilobites, fossil algae, red marble
Tools: Rock pick, collecting bag, chisel
Vehicle type: Any for trilobites, four-wheel drive for marble
Special attractions: None
Maps: USGS Cadiz Summit
For more information: BLM Desert Access Guide Providence Mountains #12
and Sheephole Mountains #15
Lore: Fossils, also called draconites and witch stones, were believed to enhance
longevity.
Finding the site: From the National Trails Highway (Old US 66) turn southeast
onto Cadiz Road. Continue on the paved road for 4.3 miles and turn left onto
a dirt road, heading in a northerly direction for 0.7 mile. (Ignore the road on
the right at 0.4 mile.) At 0.7 mile turn onto the dirt road to your right. At 0.2
mile stay left and continue another 0.8 mile. You will see black buttes ahead.
The fossils are located by walking up the road to several shale deposits. The
thick shale pieces can be "opened" to reveal trilobite casts and molds by turning the shale on end and gently tapping the edge. The shale will split, revealing
a trilobite form.

A 4x4 will be needed to get to the marble site, reached by driving a sandy
wash. From the fossil site backtrack to the 0.2-mile mark, where a dirt road
took off to the right in a northeasterly direction. Drive this road for 1.1 miles;
turn left at the rock cairn and drive up out of the wash, following the road to
the small marble quarry ahead.

Rockhounding

The fossil trilobite site has long been a favorite of rockhounds, with an abundant supply of casts and molds of these ancient sea creatures. However, the fossil
shales have been mined and most have been removed. It is still possible to find
fossil trilobites by sifting through the broken shale left by the miners. Fossil

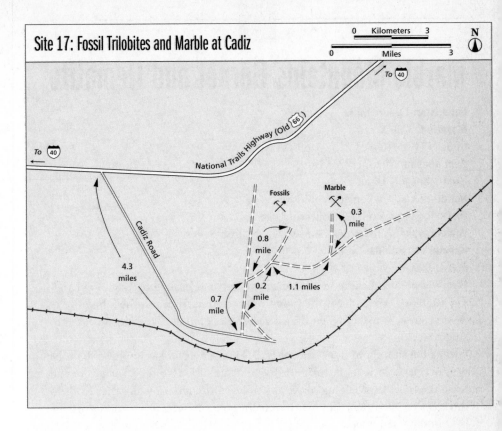

Site 17: Fossil Trilobites and Marble at Cadiz

algae are found in this area as well. Look for a gray stone with black whorls; this is the fossil algae.

The red marble site yields a moderate-grade marble in a deep burgundy red or white with red flecks. You will need a 4x4 to get to this site, as access is through a sandy wash.

Marble Mountains Garnet and Hematite

Land type: Desert hills
Elevation: 1,200 feet
GPS: N34 35.76' / W115 31.89'
Best season: October to May
Land manager: BLM
Material: Garnet, hematite, epidote
Tools: Rock pick, chisel, collecting bag
Vehicle type: Sturdy truck or four-wheel drive
Special attractions: None
Maps: USGS Cadiz
Lore: Garnet was believed to enhance strength and healing by way of enhancing the blood. Hematite is the bloodstone referred to in the Bible because of the red streak it makes when drawn across tile. Epidote, like jade, was used to attract wealth.
Finding the site: From the National Trails Highway (Old US 66) head 0.3 mile west of the Cadiz turnoff. Turn north (right) and drive 0.5 mile. Turn right and drive 0.3 mile. Turn left and drive 2.3 miles north, ignoring all other roads to the right or left. A small brown mountain contains seams of garnets, particularly in the open pockets.

Rockhounding

This site offers small to large garnets of pink, red, and brown. The small garnets are suitable for faceting, while the large ones, left in matrix, make great display pieces. The large garnets are too fractured and opaque to make nice faceted gems. Use your chisel to remove the garnet-containing matrix. Also sift through the dirt at the bottom of the pockets for loose garnets.

The green, platy stone scattered about is epidote. Epidote has no

Grapefruit-size rock coated in garnets.
PHOTO BY SHEP KOSS

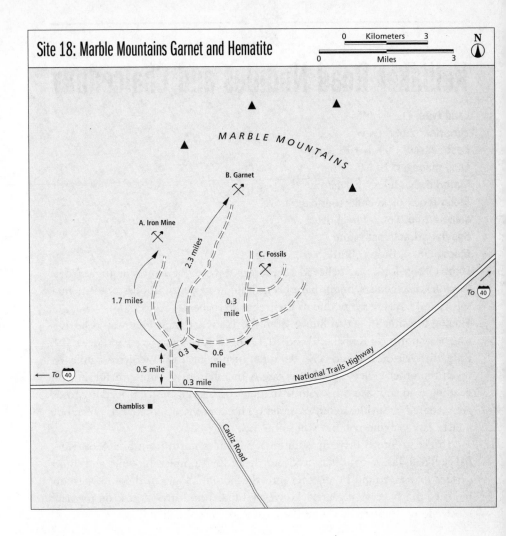

0   Kilometers   3

0   Miles   3

N

MARBLE MOUNTAINS

B. Garnet

A. Iron Mine

2.3 miles

C. Fossils

1.7 miles

0.3 mile

To 40

0.3

0.6 mile

0.5 mile

To 40

0.3 mile

National Trails Highway

Chambliss

Cadiz Road

jewelry value, but as one of the eight earth-forming minerals, it makes a nice addition to a serious mineral collection.

Much of the epidote contains blades of metallic hematite, also desirable for mineral collectors. Larger chunks of hematite found in the area are suitable for lapidary uses.

Kelbaker Road Nodules and Chalcedony

Land type: Desert hills
Elevation: 2,600 feet
Best season: October to April
Land manager: BLM
Material: Nodules, chalcedony
Tools: Rock pick, collecting bag, shovel
Vehicle type: Four-wheel drive
Special attractions: None
Maps: USGS Brown Buttes and Amboy

Lore: Chalcedony was believed to protect travelers and prevent nightmares. Nodules, like geodes, might have been thought to be the abodes of elemental spirits and female energy due to their egglike shapes.

Finding the site: To get to Site A from the National Trails Highway (Old US 66), head north on Kelbaker Road. At 1.6 miles turn right (east) and drive 0.1 mile. Turn left (north) and drive 0.9 mile. Turn right (east) and drive 1 mile. To reach the other collecting areas at Site A merely return 1 mile to the north-heading road and take other faintly marked roads going east. Chalcedony roses are scattered about the desert pavement. The concentrations are not great, but a little easy walking will net you some nice specimens.

To get to Site B drive an additional 5.7 miles north from Site A on Kelbaker Road. Take a road that heads northeast for 1.6 miles. Nodules and some geodes may be found by digging into the hillside. Some of these geodes are reported to have crystal centers. However, I didn't find any of those on my trip. Chalcedony is scattered around the areas at the base of the hill.

Rockhounding

Rockhounds visited this site extensively in the past. However, there haven't been many trips to this area in recent years. The scarcity of activity, as well as erosion by wind and rain, has allowed the area to accumulate more material for rockhounds to collect.

The aforementioned processes of erosion have not improved the road to Site B. It is recommended that you use a 4x4 to reach this site.

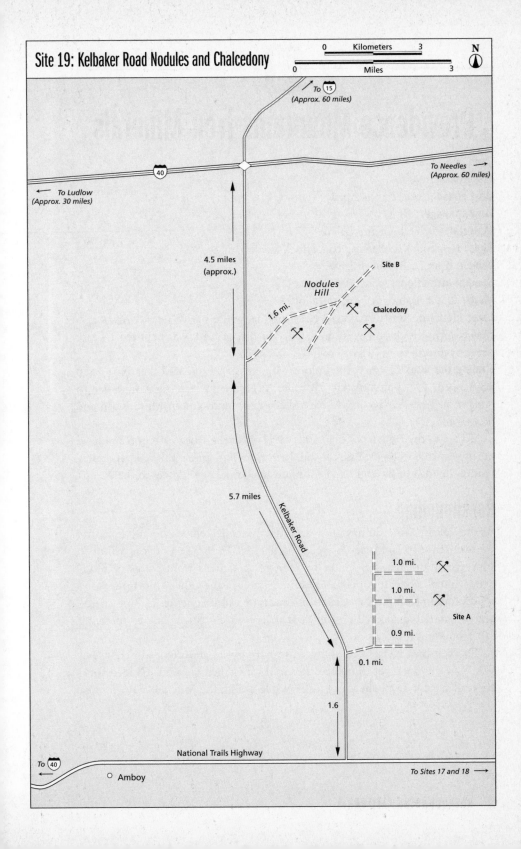

Site 19: Kelbaker Road Nodules and Chalcedony

Kilometers
0 3

Miles
0 3

N

To 15
(Approx. 60 miles)

40

To Needles →
(Approx. 60 miles)

← To Ludlow
(Approx. 30 miles)

4.5 miles
(approx.)

Nodules
Hill

Site B

1.6 mi.

Chalcedony

5.7 miles

Kelbaker Road

1.0 mi.

1.0 mi.

0.9 mi.

Site A

0.1 mi.

1.6

National Trails Highway

To 40

Amboy

To Sites 17 and 18 →

Providence Mountains Iron Minerals

Land type: Desert hills
Elevation: 2,600 feet
Best season: October to April
Land manager: BLM
Material: Pyrite, hematite, galena
Tools: Rock pick, collecting bag, chisel, crack hammer
Vehicle type: Four-wheel drive
Special attractions: Mitchell Caverns
Maps: USGS Fountain Peak and Colton Well
Lore: Hematite was thought to cure anemia, while pyrite was worn or carried to bring luck and wealth. Galena, an ore of lead, was believed to ease nervous disorders.
Finding the site: To reach the Vulcan Mine, exit I-40 at Kelbaker Road and head north for approximately 18 miles. (Be sure to bear right in order to remain on Kelbaker Road.) Make a sharp right onto Vulcan Mine Road and drive 5 miles.

To get to the Bonanza King Mine, exit I-40 at the Essex off-ramp and head northwest 10.8 miles on Essex Road. Turn right and follow this road 4.7 miles. Ignore the road to the right and continue an additional 1.9 miles to the dumps.

Rockhounding

At the Vulcan Mine dumps, iron ores may be collected. Pyrite and hematite are of interest to lapidaries as well as collectors. In some cases you will need your chisel and crack hammer to remove specimens from seams in boulders. Mineral collectors may also be interested in the other colorful red and yellow mining by-products, such as limonite and magnetite. Epidote is the green material and may be of interest to collectors, as it is one of the eight earth-building minerals.

The Bonanza King Mine dumps also have pyrite and the lead ore, galena. While in this area, you must see the nearby Mitchell Caverns. Guided tours are available. Do not collect any fossils while within the Mitchell Caverns area.

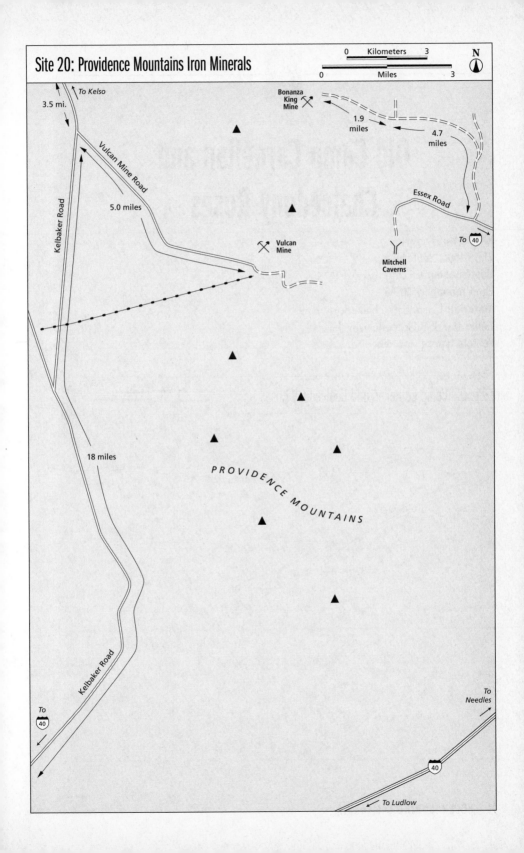

Site 20: Providence Mountains Iron Minerals

To Kelso

3.5 mi.

Vulcan Mine Road

Kelbaker Road

5.0 miles

Vulcan Mine

Bonanza King Mine

1.9 miles

4.7 miles

Essex Road

To 40

Mitchell Caverns

18 miles

PROVIDENCE MOUNTAINS

Kelbaker Road

To 40

To Needles

40

To Ludlow

0   Kilometers   3

0   Miles   3

N

Old Camp Carnelian and Chalcedony Roses

Land type: Desert
Elevation: 1,450 feet
Best season: October to April
Land manager: BLM
Material: Carnelian, chalcedony roses
Tools: Rock pick, collecting bag
Vehicle type: Four-wheel drive

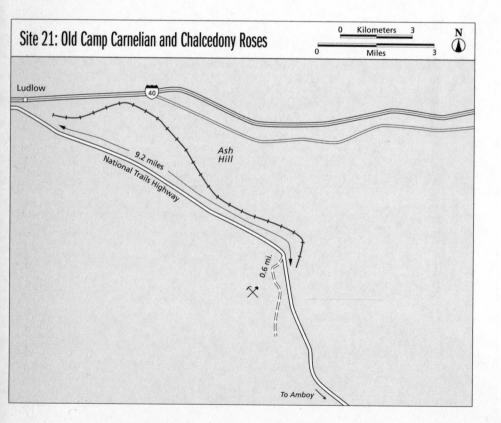

Site 21: Old Camp Carnelian and Chalcedony Roses

Ludlow

40

Ash Hill

9.2 miles
National Trails Highway

0.6 mi.

To Amboy

Special attractions: None

Maps: USGS Ash Hill

Lore: Carnelian brought protection and peace; chalcedony roses would likely have the same attributes as plain chalcedony: protection from nightmares and protection for travelers.

Finding the site: From Ludlow drive 9.2 miles east on the National Trails Highway (Old US 66). Turn right and drive 0.6 mile to the site.

Rockhounding

At this site you will find carnelian, a type of agate, in translucent to opaque cream, yellow, orange, and orange-red. The road has not been maintained for some time and was very washed out during my visit. Near the collecting area you will see remains of an old camp.

Ludlow Gems

Land type: Desert
Elevation: 1,980 feet
Best season: October to May
Land manager: BLM
Material: Jasper, agate, manganese, calcite, copper minerals
Tools: Rock pick, collecting bag
Vehicle type: Four-wheel drive
Special attractions: None
Maps: USGS Broadwell Dry Lake and Ludlow
Lore: Jasper and agate bring courage and strength. In New Age philosophies, manganese ores are believed to enhance psychic development. Calcite was thought to assist in purifying the body during fasting. Copper and its minerals were used to enhance healing and the growth of plants.

Brick-size multicolored agate. Photo by Shep Koss

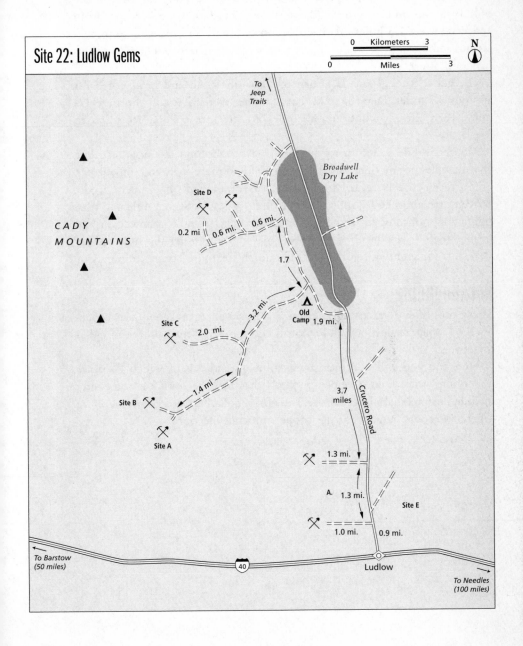

Site 22: Ludlow Gems

0   Kilometers   3
0   Miles   3

N

To Jeep Trails

Broadwell Dry Lake

CADY MOUNTAINS

Site D

0.2 mi   0.6 mi.   0.6 mi.

1.7

3.2 mi.

Old Camp

1.9 mi.

Site C   2.0 mi.

1.4 mi

Site B

Site A

3.7 miles

Crucero Road

1.3 mi.

A.   1.3 mi.

Site E

1.0 mi.   0.9 mi.

To Barstow
(50 miles)

40

Ludlow

To Needles
(100 miles)

Finding the site: From Ludlow head north 0.9 mile on Crucero Road. Turn left and head west 1 mile. Here you will find jasper along the base of the hills. Back out on Crucero Road, continue 1.3 miles farther; turn left again and drive west 1.3 miles. At this location you will find manganese minerals and some calcite in seams. There's some jasper here too. These locations make up Site E.

To get to sites A and B return to Crucero Road and head north for another 3.7 miles. Take the road that branches to the left and continue 1.9 miles. Turn left and continue 3.2 miles. At the fork, go left 1.4 miles to find agate.

To get to Site C return to the fork at 1.4 miles, and this time go right. Drive 2 miles on the right fork; here you will find more agate and some jasper.

To reach Site D return to the road that branched off Crucero Road. Drive north another 1.7 miles and turn left (west). Drive 0.6 mile and turn right. For more copper minerals, return to the 0.6-mile point again and turn onto the west-heading road. You may drive another 0.6 mile farther west, turning right and going 0.2 mile north for more copper minerals.

Rockhounding

These sites offer a variety of colorful agate, as well as moss and lace varieties. Red jasper, chalcedony, and colorful common opal may also be found at these sites.

Here too you will find manganese minerals and calcite, which fluoresce under ultraviolet light. Copper minerals that may be found at these sites include bornite, malachite, cuprite, and chrysocolla. There is also some more calcite and some hematite at the copper minerals location.

West of Ludlow Chalcedony, Calcite, and More

Land type: Desert
Elevation: 1,900 feet
Best season: October to April
Land manager: BLM
Material: Colorful jasper, agate, chalcedony, calcite
Tools: Rock pick, collecting bag
Vehicle type: Four-wheel drive
Special attractions: None
Maps: USGS Ludlow and Broadwell Dry Lake
Lore: Jasper, agate, and chalcedony all have protective qualities. Calcite was worn to assist the purification of the body during fasting.
Finding the site: You can access this site by driving west of Ludlow on the National Trails Highway (Old US 66) for 3.6 miles. This will put you at the first turnoff to one of many sites with plentiful collecting material. Head north and follow the mileages given on the accompanying map to reach the varied collecting areas.

To reach additional sites you may continue an additional 1.5 miles on the National Trails Highway and head north, following the mileages on the map.

Rockhounding

This site, with its varied collecting spots and colorful material, has long been a favorite of rockhounds. The material is still plentiful in most places. The agate and jasper are colorful, in reds, yellows, greens, and oranges, with black and brown banding.

Check boulder seams in all locations for calcite crystallizing in the rhombohedral form.

This area is reputed to have rainbow jasper and Iceland spar. Even though I did not find any, you might. I did not linger long enough to do the area full justice. A day is just not enough to fully cover the area, so plan to spend several days if you can.

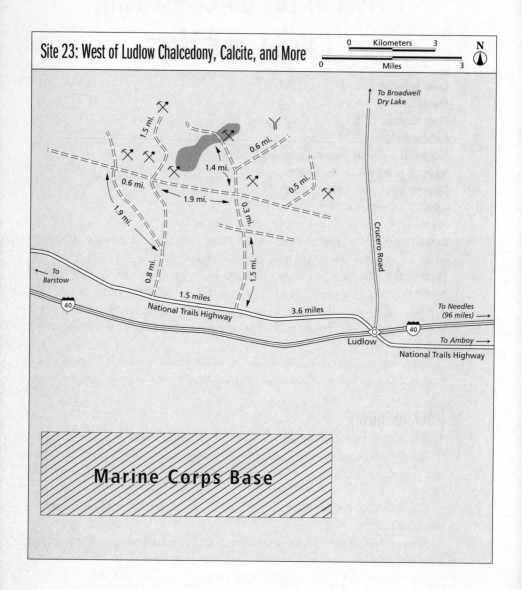

Site 23: West of Ludlow Chalcedony, Calcite, and More

Kilometers

Miles

N

To Broadwell
Dry Lake

1.5 mi.

0.6 mi.

1.4 mi.

0.6 mi.

0.5 mi.

1.9 mi.

0.3 mi.

1.9 mi.

0.8 mi.

1.5 mi.

Crucero Road

To
Barstow

40

National Trails Highway

1.5 miles

3.6 miles

To Needles
(96 miles) →

40

Ludlow

To Amboy →

National Trails Highway

Marine Corps Base

Hector Agates and Jasper

Land type: Desert hills
Elevation: 2,004 feet
Best season: October to April
Land manager: BLM
Material: Agate, jasper
Tools: Rock pick, collecting bag, rake
Vehicle type: Four-wheel drive
Special attractions: Pisgah Crater volcanic tube exploration
Maps: USGS Hector and Sunshine Peak
Lore: Agate and jasper were believed to bring courage, strength, and protection. Jasper was used by Native Americans to bring rain.

Hector agate with inclusions. PHOTO BY SHEP KOSS

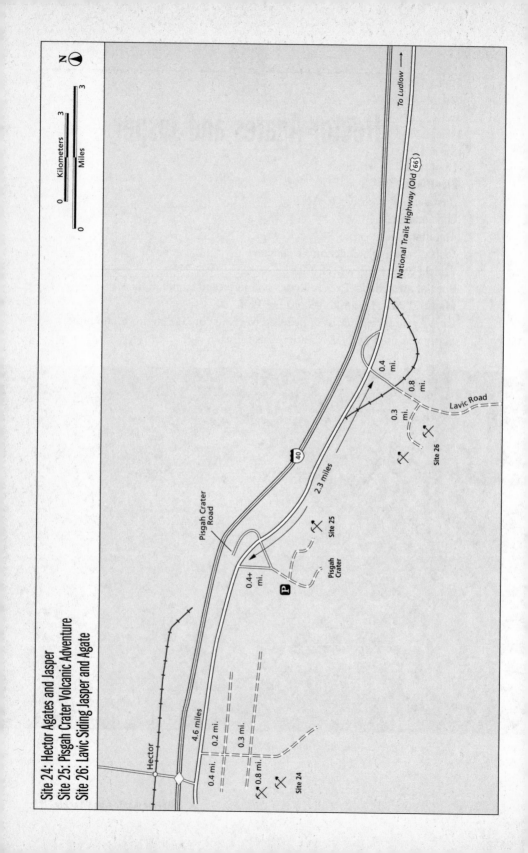

Site 24: Hector Agates and Jasper
Site 25: Pisgah Crater Volcanic Adventure
Site 26: Lavic Siding Jasper and Agate

Finding the site: On the National Trails Highway (Old US 66), drive 0.4 mile east of the Hector turnoff. Turn right (south) off the National Trails Highway and drive 0.2 mile, ignoring the gas line road that crosses the road you are on. Drive an additional 0.3 mile and turn right (west); continue for 0.8 mile. Do not drive off the road; the area is very sandy.

Rockhounding

This site is an old favorite of rockhounds. Consequently, much material has been gathered over the years. Still some remains available to the rockhound willing to do some walking about. The farther you walk, the more you will collect. Bring your lunch, spend the day, and plan to get some exercise. A rake will enable you to gather those pieces that are lying unseen just beneath the sandy surface. If you plan your trip after desert storms, your search will be easier because more material will be freshly exposed. This is a good area to visit as part of a weeklong trip while visiting other collecting sites in this area.

In addition to the agate, you may collect jasper here, as well as occasional pieces of chalcedony and some common opal.

Pisgah Crater Volcanic Adventure

(See map on page 82.)

Land type: Desert plateau basalts
Elevation: 2,100 feet
Best season: October to April
Land manager: BLM
Material: Volcanic bombs, lava rock, goethite
Tools: Rock pick, collecting bag, flashlights, gloves, hard hat, hiking shoes
Vehicle type: Any
Special attractions: None
Maps: USGS Sunshine Peak and Lavic Lake
Lore: Volcanic rocks of all types are associated with the Hawaiian goddess Pele. Because of lava's supposed powers of protection and magic, altars and temples were built from it. Holding a stone containing goethite was supposed to enable one to hear the "music of the spheres."
Finding the site: Exit I-40 at Hector Road and onto the National Trails Highway. Drive east 4.6 miles on the National Trails Highway until you come to a paved road to your right. This is Pisgah Crater Road, and you will see a sign indicating Twin Mountain Rock Company. Turn right and proceed for 0.4-plus mile to a closed gate. Park on the road to the right of the gate. Walk beyond the gate and along the road for a short distance, looking for a footpath heading east from the road. Follow this footpath as it heads around Pisgah's volcanic crater and through a massive lava field, or basalt plateau. When you are on the east side of the crater, begin walking over the lava field. You will encounter the openings to many volcanic tubes. The walk to the tubes is approximately 0.75 mile from the paved road.

Rockhounding

Pisgah Crater has been the site of commercial mining activity for many years. The volcanic rock is used to manufacture paving material and for use as briquettes in electric and gas barbecues.

You may look down into the bowl of the crater from its east side at the lava tube field, but the most interesting feature is the lava field itself. Here you can collect volcanic bombs that were ejected thousands of years ago during long-ago eruptions. Look for football-shaped rocks of varying sizes. Some of the lava

Painted hills such as these sometimes contain interesting fossils.
Photo by Garret Romaine

rock is coated with metallic goethite in colors of gold, blue, and violet. Most of this goethite coating seems to be found near the parking area.

The volcanic lava tubes beckon to the adventurous. These are located on the easternmost side of Pisgah. There are a variety of openings; some are easier than others to enter. There are tubes to match most adventure levels.

The tubes are a labyrinth of interesting tunnels and rooms. Within the tubes is a register you may wish to sign and date to mark the fact that you were there.

Wearing gloves while climbing in the tubes will protect your hands. A hard hat is recommended but not essential. Take a couple flashlights, extra batteries and bulbs, and a canteen of water. Above all, be careful.

The walk from the paved road to the tubes is about 0.75 mile. Some of the trek will take you through deep sand and over low, steep hills. Good hiking boots are recommended.

This is a good spot to see pahoehoe (pronounced *pa-hoy-hoy*) type lava flow. The Hawaiian people are familiar with volcanic eruptions and have words for describing the various types of lava. Geologists and volcanologists have adopted these descriptive words.

Pahoehoe describes a thick, viscous lava that shows flow marks, ripples, and ropey coils. This is what you will see at Pisgah. The other type is "aa" (pronounced *ah-ah*). Aa describes a less-viscous type of lava that cools into blocks, columns, or jagged cinders.

If you take this trip on a weekend, you will likely see groups of students camped along the road below the gate, as well as a bus or two parked near the gate. Pisgah is the pilgrimage site to which geology teachers from all over the state bring their students to study the mechanics of volcanism and explore the tubes. This is how I took my first volcanic-tube adventure, while studying geology at Chaffee College with Rod Parcel. I later reprised this trip with partners Mo and Ed Hemler.

The parking area near the gate is also a great place to collect replacement briquettes for your barbecue.

Lavic Siding Jasper and Agate

(See map on page 82.)
Land type: Desert
Elevation: 1,900 feet
GPS: N34 42.795' / W116 19.408'
Best season: October to April
Land manager: BLM
Material: Colorful jasper and agate
Tools: Rock pick, collecting bag
Vehicle type: Four-wheel drive

Brecciated and ribbon Lavic jasper. PHOTO BY SHEP KOSS

Special attractions: Pisgah Crater volcanic tube exploration
For more information: USGS Sunshine Peak and Lavic Lake
Lore: Warriors carried jasper and agate for strength and courage.
Finding the site: *Note:* The crossing of Lavic Road over the railroad tracks is no longer available. Continue west on the National Trails Highway from Ludlow for 10 miles to where the railroad tracks cross the highway. Just south of the tracks turn left onto the railroad maintenance road and head east for about 1.5 miles back to Lavic Road, which is the first main graded road to the right. Turn right; travel this road for about 1 mile and park. Do not turn onto any of the side roads unless in a high-clearance 4x4, as many are sandy. Collecting in this area is widespread. Do not travel much farther south than 1 mile on Lavic Road from the railroad tracks, as this area borders an off-limits military base. The military has a large sign posting the boundary. *Caution: This base is a weapons test site. Avoid any large cylindrical objects, which may be unexploded ordnance.*

Rockhounding

Although this site is an old rockhound favorite, good material still remains. Here you can collect colorful jasper and agate in reds, blues, vibrant yellows, and oranges. Some of this material has showy white banding. Walk out into the desert, especially toward the west, and you may find more and larger pieces.

West of Hector Blue Chalcedony, Jasper, and Agate

Land type: Desert
Elevation: 1,900 feet
GPS: N34 46.985' / W116 30.462'
Best season: October to April
Land manager: BLM
Material: Blue chalcedony, colorful agate, jasper
Tools: Rock pick, collecting bag
Vehicle type: Four-wheel drive
Special attractions: Pisgah Crater volcanic tube exploration

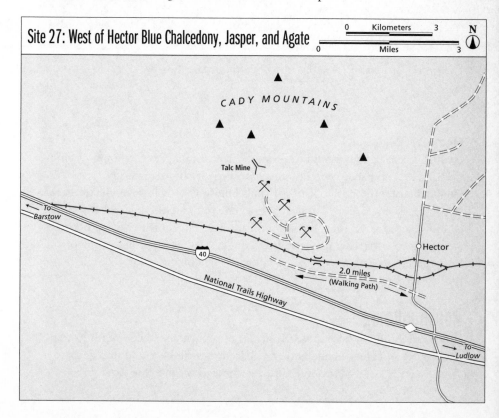

Site 27: West of Hector Blue Chalcedony, Jasper, and Agate

Orange, red, and brown Hector hills jasper. Photo by Shep Koss

Maps: USGS Hector
Lore: Blue chalcedony is said to promote sleep, healing, and calming of emotions. Agate and jasper were the stones of warriors and rainmakers.
Finding the site: From the National Trails Highway or I-40, take Hector Road
north for approximately 1 mile. Park where you can; the railroad has closed
all crossings, so travel must be on foot from here on. Go left (west) for 2 miles
along the road paralleling the railroad tracks. The material lies north of the
tracks and mostly up on an orange-colored hill, which is about 0.5 mile north
of the railroad tracks.

Rockhounding

Jasper can be found here in warm shades of orange and yellow with banding
in a variety of colors, including red. Chalcedony will be found in blue as well
as many other colors. However, this site is prized for the blue variety.

Newberry Nodules

Land type: Desert hills
Elevation: 1,970 feet
GPS: N34 48.20' / W116 40.25'
Best season: October to April
Land manager: BLM
Material: Agate-filled nodules
Tools: Rock pick, collecting bag, shovel
Vehicle type: Four-wheel drive
Special attractions: None
Maps: USGS Newberry Springs
Lore: Nodules, like geodes, were thought to be the abode of elemental spirits.
Finding the site: Exit I-40 at Memorial Drive and head west 3 miles on the National Trails Highway, or exit at Newberry Springs and head east on the National Trails Highway for 2.1 miles. Turn south onto Newberry Road and drive 0.6 mile. Veer right, ignoring Magney Lane, and drive 1 mile to the quarry. Even with a 4x4, you may want to park here and walk west to the hills.

Rockhounding

By digging into the white patches of ancient ash among the hills, you will find nodules filled with agate. Some have crystalline centers. Although these are said to be rare, I have found a few over the years.

The farther into the hills you go, the better your luck will be. This area has been visited frequently by rockhounds in past years, so plan on doing some looking and hiking about. Try to imagine where others have not looked, and you might net some nodules. Search in pockets that appear to have been well excavated; it is likely that not all the nodules were recovered in the past. I have had some luck doing this.

Be prepared to do some strenuous digging in your quest for nodules, or search the areas below the white deposits after heavy rains. This is a good time to find newly uncovered nodules or those that have eroded out of the deposits.

Site 28: Newberry Nodules

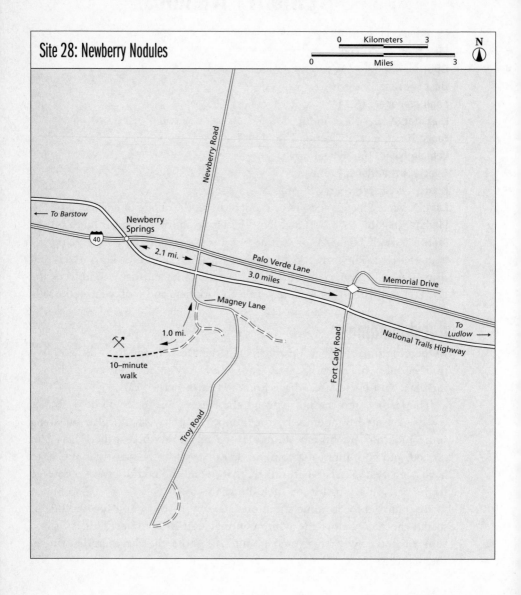

0   Kilometers   3
0   Miles   3

N

Newberry Road

← To Barstow

Newberry Springs

40

2.1 mi.

Palo Verde Lane

3.0 miles

Memorial Drive

Magney Lane

1.0 mi.

10–minute walk

Fort Cady Road

To Ludlow →

National Trails Highway

Troy Road

Orbicular Rhyolite at Grandview Mine

Land type: Desert hills
Elevation: 3,000 feet
GPS: N34 37.25' / W116 45.35'
Best season: October to April
Land manager: BLM
Material: Orbicular rhyolite
Tools: Rock pick, collecting bag
Vehicle type: Four-wheel drive
Special attractions: None
Maps: USGS Grandview Mine
Lore: Held during meditation, orbicular rhyolite was believed to assist in self-realization, corresponding to the adage "know thyself." This was perhaps due to the eyelike patterns.
Finding the site: From the junction of CA 247 and CA 18 at Lucerne Valley, drive east 5 miles. Turn left (north) onto Camp Rock Road and drive 4 miles. Veer right at the fork, remaining on Camp Rock Road. Continue northeast on Camp Rock Road for 9 miles. Turn left and drive 1 mile. The material will be scattered on the slope faces on both sides of the road in the vicinity of the Grandview Mine.

Rockhounding

Here you will find orbicular rhyolite, so named because of its eyelike patterning. This material makes excellent display pieces and is a fine addition to any mineral collection. Less-porous pieces make spectacular cabochons.

Rhyolite is a type of igneous extrusive rock. It is composed of feldspar, quartz, and amphibole, often with a few other elements that affect coloration.

The Grandview Mine is aptly named. The view from the mine is grand indeed. Be careful; there are some vertical shafts in the mine area.

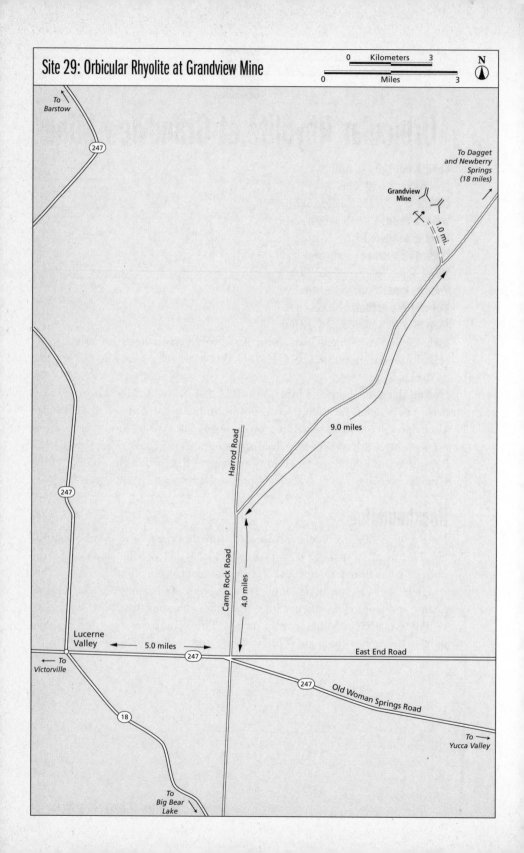

Kilometers

0   3

Miles

0   3

N

To
Barstow

247

To Dagget
and Newberry
Springs
(18 miles)

Grandview
Mine

1.0 mi.

9.0 miles

Harrod Road

Camp Rock Road

4.0 miles

Lucerne
Valley

5.0 miles

247

← To
Victorville

East End Road

247

Old Woman Springs Road

18

To →
Yucca Valley

To
Big Bear
Lake

Marble Quarry off Stoddard Wells Road

Land type: Desert mountains
Elevation: 4,200 feet
GPS: N34 40.17' / W117 05.60'
Best season: October to May
Land manager: BLM
Material: Marble
Tools: Heavy canvas bags or canvas tarp, pick, chisel, crack hammer or sledge
Vehicle type: Any
Special attractions: Roy Rogers/Dale Evans Museum
Maps: USGS Stoddard
For more information: BLM Desert Access Guide Stoddard Valley #10
Lore: Greeks and European alchemists wore or carried a chip of marble to hasten healing of broken bones and skin ailments and for its calming qualities. Marble makes an excellent "worry stone."
Finding the site: Exit I-15 at Stoddard Wells Road and head northeast for 3 miles to the railroad tracks. Cross the tracks and continue on Stoddard Wells Road for an additional 6.8 miles. Turn right onto the dirt road and drive 1.3 miles to the base of the large mountain. The mountain will show obvious lighter colored tailings near its summit. These are the tailings of the Verde Antique Marble Quarry. If you have a 4x4, you may drive part of the way up the mountain to the marble quarry. If not, park at the base and walk up the road to the quarry. The road has been partially washed out over the years. When I visited I was able to drive about one-third of the way up. The walk is about 0.3 mile. It isn't a hard walk, and the view from the quarry is positively panoramic.

Rockhounding

The Verde Antique Marble Quarry has long been a well-known collecting site for rockhounds interested in making bookends, carvings, or other projects that require sizable chunks of marble.

The quarry was renowned for its brilliant yellowish-green material, and due to its popularity, the yellowish-green marble is in short supply. Fist-size and smaller pieces can still be found, as can large chunks with flecks of the popular yellowish-green coloring. Much material in white, cream, gray, pale green,

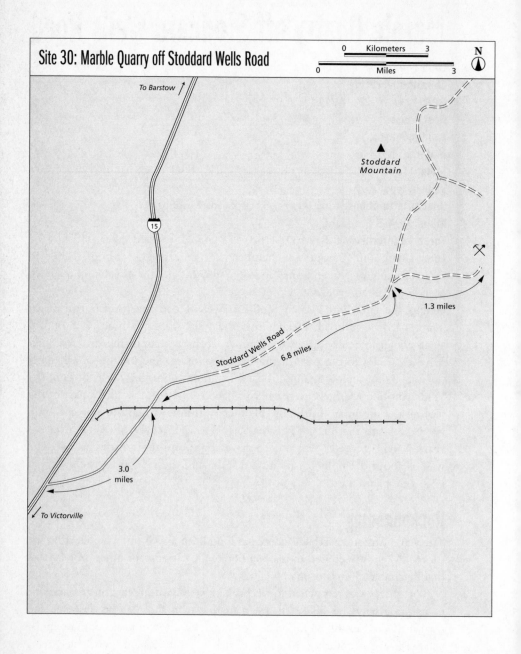

Site 30: Marble Quarry off Stoddard Wells Road

0   Kilometers   3

0   Miles   3

N

To Barstow

15

Stoddard
Mountain

1.3 miles

Stoddard Wells Road

6.8 miles

3.0
miles

To Victorville

Tricolor marble from Stoddard Wells. PHOTO BY SHEP KOSS

pink, and black can still be found in sizable chunks. Some of the material has interesting patterns of banding and veining.

There is so much material lying around that you won't have any trouble finding the size chunk you want to work up. However, bring a chisel and crack hammer along should you decide you want smaller pieces for the walk back to your vehicle. Heavy canvas bags can be filled with chunks of marble and dragged back down the mountain. A heavy canvas tarp would serve a similar purpose.

While on the mountain, I picked up a beautiful lump of jewelry-grade hematite. Although hematite wasn't abundant in the area, you may want to keep your eyes to the ground for some.

Opal Mountain Opal and Agate

Land type: Desert mountains
Elevation: 3,800 feet
GPS: N35 09.67' / W117 11.28'
Best season: October to May
Land manager: BLM
Material: Colorful common opal and agate
Tools: Rock pick, collecting bag, chisel
Vehicle type: Four-wheel drive
Special attractions: None
Maps: USGS Opal Mountain
Lore: Common opal was carried or worn to increase one's self-esteem. It was thought that with increased self-esteem, all else would follow, such as wealth, love, and contentment.
Finding the site: Take CA 58 west from Barstow and exit onto Hinkley Road. Drive north on Hinkley Road for 0.8 mile to the railroad tracks. Cross the tracks and continue another 7.5 miles. Veer right (northeast) onto Opal Mountain Road and drive 3.9 miles. Take the left-most fork, staying on Opal Mountain Road, and drive another 6.6 miles. Turn left and drive 1.4 miles to gather some jasper.

Return 1.4 miles to the main northwest road (Opal Mountain Road) and continue another 0.6 mile. Turn left and drive 0.2 mile to collect more jasper and agate if you wish. Return 0.6 mile to the main road, and go another 1.2 miles northwest. Turn right, park, and search the area for orange opal and more agate.

Return to the main road and drive 0.1 mile northwest, ignoring all roads on the left. The road straightens to almost due north. From here most roads heading to the right and left will lead to deposits of orange or green opal.

Rockhounding

Although in years past this area could be entered by two-wheel-drive vehicles, several years ago members of the Bear Gulch Rock Club and I became hopelessly mired in deep sand. My motor home, a couple trailers, and a large fifth-wheel became stuck fast. Even the four-wheel-drive tow vehicle that came from Barstow to assist us became mired. Our most welcome escape was the

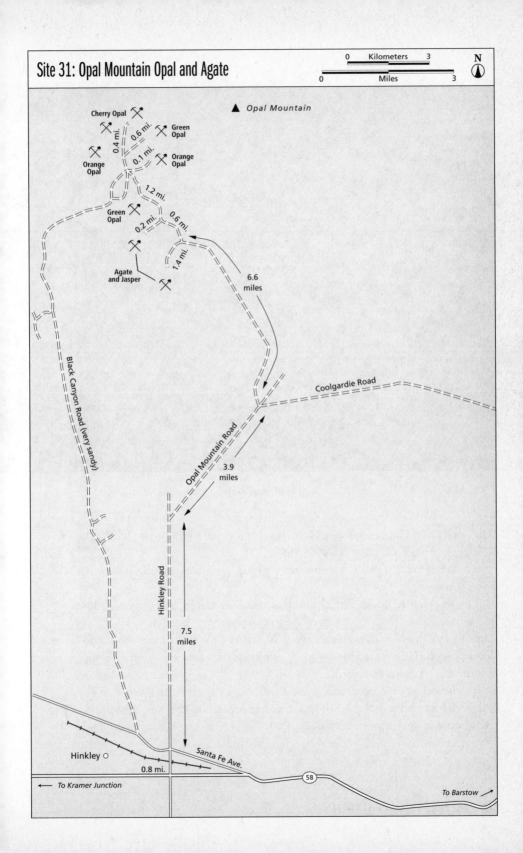

Site 31: Opal Mountain Opal and Agate

Kilometers 0 — 3

Miles 0 — 3

N

▲ Opal Mountain

Cherry Opal

0.4 mi. 0.6 mi.

Green Opal

Orange Opal

0.1 mi.

Orange Opal

1.2 mi.

Green Opal

0.2 mi. 0.6 mi.

1.4 mi.

Agate and Jasper

6.6 miles

Coolgardie Road

Black Canyon Road (very sandy)

Opal Mountain Road

3.9 miles

Hinkley Road

7.5 miles

Hinkley ○

0.8 mi.

Santa Fe Ave.

← To Kramer Junction

58

To Barstow →

Opal Mountain bubble gum rhyolite and cabachon. PHOTO BY SHEP KOSS

result of a BLM ranger who towed each and every one of us out, including the tow truck, with his Dodge Ram Charger.

I recommend a 4x4 or traveling in a group with at least one 4x4 and a good towrope.

The material here is colorful common opal in orange, red, green, yellow, and white. Although it doesn't have the fire attributed to precious opal, it does seem to be "fired" with an inner glow. It occurs in seams in the mountain's country rock. Yes, you will need to do some chisel work. Be careful though; this material is easily fractured.

If you find any red opal, you will be collecting the rare cherry opal. It can still be found in the northernmost collecting areas, but it is rare and usually found only in very thin red seams.

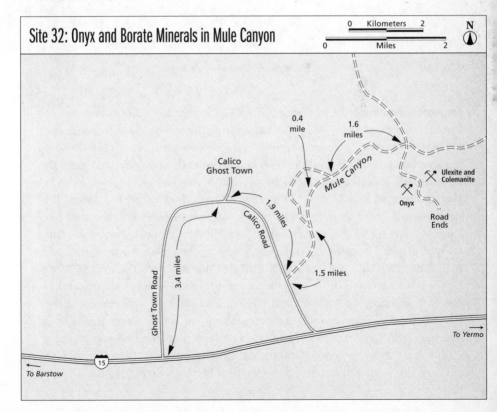

SITE 32

Onyx and Borate Minerals in Mule Canyon

Land type: Desert mountains
Elevation: 2,600 feet
Best season: October to May
Land manager: BLM
Material: Translucent, honey, and gray-banded onyx; borate minerals
Tools: Bag, rock pick
Vehicle type: Any
Special attractions: Calico Ghost Town
Maps: USGS Yermo

Site 32: Onyx and Borate Minerals in Mule Canyon

0   Kilometers   2

0   Miles   2

N

0.4 mile

1.6 miles

Mule Canyon

Calico Ghost Town

Ulexite and Colemanite

Onyx

1.9 miles

Calico Road

Road Ends

Ghost Town Road

3.4 miles

1.5 miles

15

To Yermo

To Barstow

Silver lace onyx slab from Mule Canyon. PHOTO BY SHEP KOSS

For more information: BLM Desert Access Guide Johnson Valley #11

Lore: Romans wore onyx for protection during night travels and in battle, also to lessen libidinous desires and calm worries. Egyptian and New Age beliefs assert that borates balance body systems and aid in maintaining skeletal strength, while ulexite enhances psychic sight.

Finding the site: Exit I-15 at Ghost Town Road. Head north and follow the signs 3.4 miles to Calico. Past the turnoff to the gate to Calico, the road becomes Calico Road. Pass Calico Ghost Town and continue 1.9 miles to Mule Canyon Road. The road to Mule Canyon is marked with a white post, and with some squinting you can barely read that this is indeed the road to Mule Canyon. Turn left and drive 1.5 miles, keeping right. Travel an additional 0.4-plus mile, still keeping to your right. Continue another 1.6 miles in an easterly direction, ignoring the road to the right. When you see the large gray tailings pile, turn right into the wash. If you are in a two-wheel-drive vehicle, you may want to park prior to driving into the narrow, shallow wash. Parts of this wash are very sandy. After about 500 feet, the wash becomes extremely narrow and peters out.

Rockhounding

Twenty feet or so up the wash from the gray tailings pile, and on the other side of the road, beautiful translucent chunks of onyx can be found. Some are beige and unremarkable, but the honey-colored onyx with gray, brown, and black banding is exquisite and would make beautiful jewelry and carvings. Onyx takes a high polish and has a satiny smooth feel when finished. Perhaps this is why onyx is made into "worry stones," those half-dollar-size pieces with thumbprint-size depressions that people carry in their pocket and rub when feeling anxious or stressed.

On the gray tailings pile in the wash and on the other side of the wash, small specimens of borate minerals, ulexite, and colemanite (TV rock) are found.

Driving into Mule Canyon you will marvel at the coloring of the surrounding hills. The mineralization of the area creates this peculiar coloring of green, yellow, and maroon. You may want to take your camera in order to capture this unusual coloration. Miners seeing this atypical coloring prospected the area in the late 1800s. Silver and gold were mined until the 1920s, when the miners began to drift off to richer digs.

Calico was restored by Walter Knott of Knott's Berry Farm fame. Knott was not only an entrepreneur but also worked the Calico mines in 1910. When you see the varicolored hills, you will understand how Calico earned its name, for the hills are as colorful as a calico quilt. There is a fee to tour the old town of Calico.

Hilltop Agate and Jasper at Mineola Road

Land type: Desert hills
Elevation: 2,100 feet
GPS: N36 56.590' / W116 46.273'
Best season: October to May
Land manager: BLM
Material: Colorful translucent agate and red jasper
Tools: Rock bag, pick
Vehicle type: Any
Special attractions: Early Man Site
Maps: USGS Yermo
For more information: BLM Desert Access Guide Johnson Valley #11 and Irwin #8
Lore: Greeks and Romans wore agate for protection, strength, and courage. Jasper was worn to aid one in breaking bad habits and was used by Native Americans in rainmaking rites.
Finding the site: From Barker travel north on I-15 and exit at Mineola Road. Turn right and drive 0.6 mile to a well-graded dirt road marked with a sign for the Early Man Site and the county dump. Drive north several hundred feet to the end of the road. Take the faint dirt road to the left 0.2 mile to the top of the hill next to the dump. The road to the top of the hill is rocky, and it is recommended that two-wheel-drive vehicles ascend the hill in low gear. You can also walk up the hill.

Rockhounding

This site is right off the freeway and easy to get to. The agate found at this location comes in most of the usual colors and is generally fist size. Red jasper in various shades abounds, and there's an occasional chalcedony rose.

If you visit the agate location Wednesday through Saturday, you may wish to stop at the Early Man archaeological site. Between 9 a.m. and 4 p.m. you can see some of the tools and other artifacts crafted by the ancient peoples who lived in this area as early as the Pleistocene epoch.

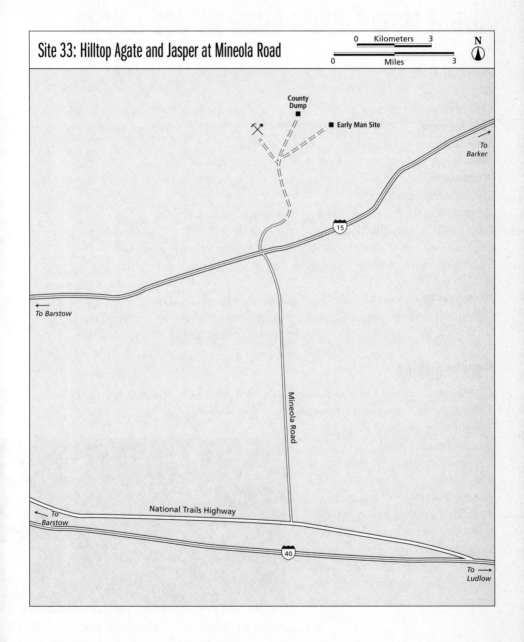

Site 33: Hilltop Agate and Jasper at Mineola Road

0   Kilometers   3

0   Miles   3

N

County
Dump

■ Early Man Site

To
Barker

15

To Barstow

Mineola Road

National Trails Highway

To
Barstow

40

To
Ludlow

Alvord Mine Copper Minerals and Calcite

Land type: Desert hills
Elevation: 3,900 feet
GPS: N35 04.17' / W116 37.62'
Best season: October to April
Land manager: BLM
Material: Chrysocolla, malachite, calcite crystals
Tools: Rock pick, collecting bag, chisel, shovel or rake
Vehicle type: Any
Special attractions: None
Maps: USGS Alvord Mountain East and Alvord Mountain West
Lore: Held in the palm of the hand, chrysocolla was thought to alleviate fear and bring peace. If danger threatened, it was believed that malachite would break into pieces, thereby warning its owner. Calcite was worn during fasting to aid cleansing of the body.
Finding the site: From I-15 or Yermo Road, take Alvord Road northwest for 2.7 miles. Pass under the power line and continue another 2.7 miles. Ignore the road to the right and drive another 0.8 mile. Turn right and go 0.4 mile to the mine.

Rockhounding

On the dumps of the old Alvord Mine you can find chrysocolla and malachite suitable for displaying and adding to mineral collections. Dig into the dumps and you may net small pieces suitable for lapidary work.

Calcite crystals in white and with a bluish tint may be found on the dumps and in seams on boulders. Agate, hematite, petrified wood, and jasper may also be collected in the area.

The Alvord gold mine hasn't been in operation for many years, but that may change as the price of gold rises and the costs of production drop.

Alvord Mine malachite and azurite chunk.
Photo by Shep Koss

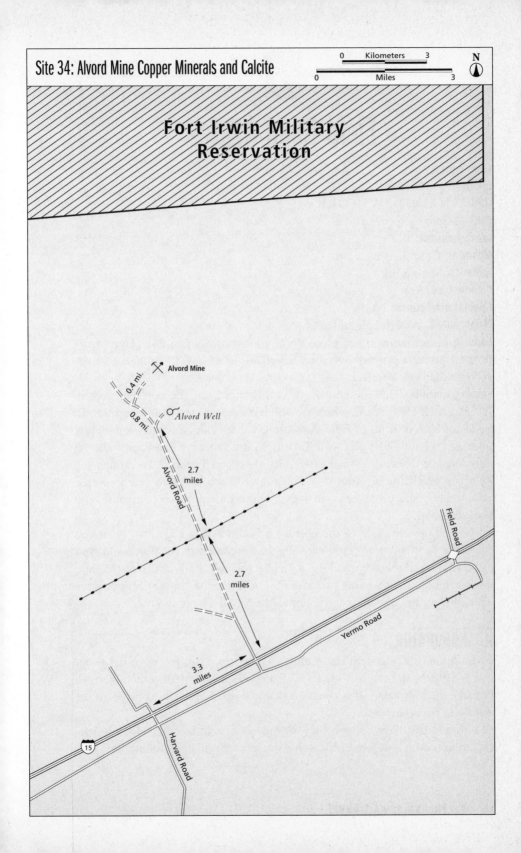

0   Kilometers   3

0   Miles   3

N

Fort Irwin Military
Reservation

Alvord Mine

0.4 mi.

0.8 mi.

Alvord Well

Alvord Road

2.7
miles

2.7
miles

Field Road

Yermo Road

3.3
miles

Harvard Road

15

Field Road Agates

Land type: Desert
Elevation: 1,600 feet
GPS: N34 59.857' / W116 01.364'
Best season: October to May
Land manager: BLM
Material: Colorful small agate
Tools: Collecting bag
Vehicle type: Any
Special attractions: None
Maps: USGS Alvord East and Dunn
Lore: Worn for courage and protection by many ancient cultures, jasper (particularly green jasper) was worn by Egyptians for its healing properties, especially of the digestive tract.
Finding the site: This site consists of two locations on the opposite sides of I-15, both off Field Road, which we will label as Location A and Location B.

Location A is south of Field Road. To get there exit I-15 and head slightly southeast 0.1 mile to a dirt road. Turn right onto this dirt road and head 0.2 mile into the desert to a small desert varnish–covered mound. In another 0.3 mile you will come to another small mound. Both these areas are covered with tumbler-size pieces of agate in gray, white, brown, and cream, some with black banding.

On the opposite side of the freeway is Location B, an agate area that you may want to spend more time enjoying. In fact, take a picnic lunch and your camera. To reach this site exit I-15 at Field Road and head northwest 0.6 mile, staying right until you come to a gas line road. Here the road forks three ways. Take the left fork and drive 1.5 miles to the top of a large mound.

Rockhounding

At Location A, along with the tumbler-size agates, small pieces of red jasper and petrified wood can be found. This is a good quick trip for tumbling rough to make the kids happy. It is also a quick and convenient stop to make on the way to or from Las Vegas.

Location B is covered with palm-size pieces of translucent agate in brown, tan, cream, and white, as well as varying shades of green. I also found some nice

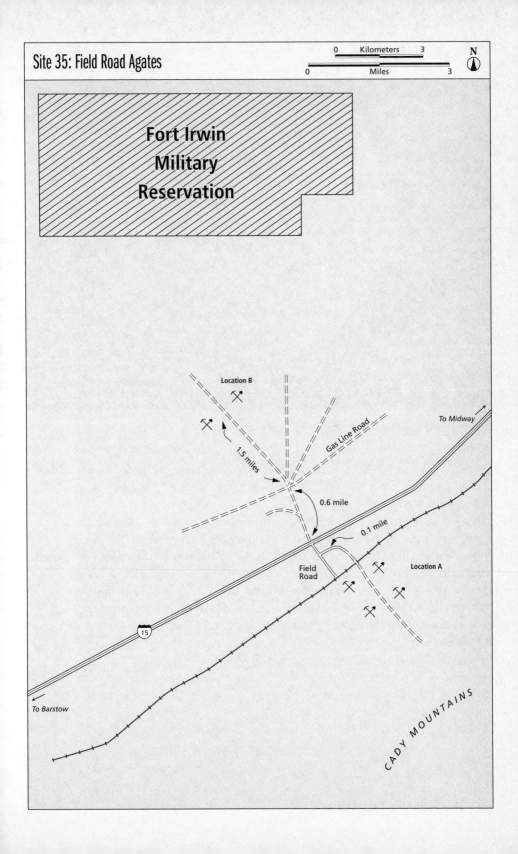

Multicolored Field Road agate. PHOTO BY SHEP KOSS

pieces of green and red jasper. Red jasper is plentiful here. I also found one, and only one, nice piece of fire agate. I suspect that some rockhound visiting the site must have accidently dropped it.

Pack a picnic lunch and plan to spend some time at this site enjoying the view of vast open spaces and distant mountain ranges. Bring a camera; the view is spectacular. There is no shade here, so picnic in the shade created by your vehicle or plan brunch instead of lunch to take advantage of cooler morning temperatures. The desert-varnished rock at this site is thick and at first appears to obscure from view the lovely agates to be found here. Within moments your eyes will become accustomed to seeing the agate and jasper against the black, varnished rocks.

Afton Canyon Collectibles

Land type: Desert canyons
Elevation: 1,600 feet
GPS: N35 02.28' / W116 23.06'
Best season: October to May
Land manager: BLM
Material: Red and yellow jasper, agate, opalite, calcite rhombs
Tools: Pick, collecting bag
Vehicle type: Any
Special attractions: Afton Canyon geography
Maps: USGS Dunn and Cave Mountain
For more information: BLM Desert Access Guide Johnson Valley #11 and Irwin #8
Lore: Opalite is reputed to have protective as well as calming qualities.
Finding the site: From I-15 east of Barstow, take the Afton Canyon off-ramp and head southeast for 3.5 miles to the second BLM campground, which will be on your left. The collecting areas consist of three canyons opposite the BLM campground.

In dry years you may walk under the train trestle, visible from camp, ford the shallow Mojave River, and head into one of three canyons. During one visit, recent and heavy rainfall caused the Mojave River to swell greatly, preventing collectors from crossing under the trestle due to a widening of the river and deep, viscous mud. Instead we had to climb 60 feet down the precipitous rock riprap that protects the railbed from erosion by the Mojave River. Once down we were able to walk northwest about 200 feet to where the river narrowed and some well-placed boulders allowed for a dry crossing.

The brush on the canyon side of the Mojave River is impenetrable and must be circumnavigated. This will bring you to face the center and largest of the canyons. All three canyons are reportedly good for collecting, and rockhounds have their favorites. My favorite is the center canyon.

Rockhounding

In years past rockhounds could drive (a 4x4 only) across the shallow Mojave River right into the canyon. Due to environmental destruction by off-road vehicles, the BLM has fenced off the canyons. You still can walk into the

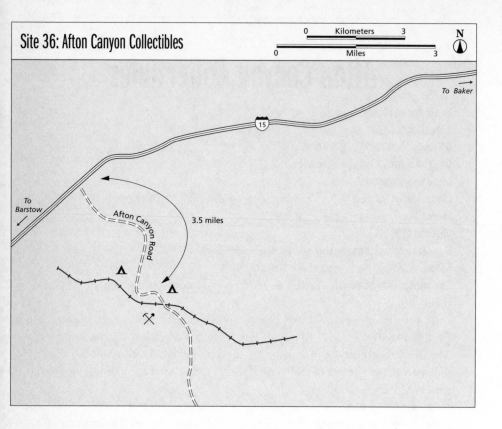

Kilometers

Miles

To Baker

To Barstow

Afton Canyon Road

3.5 miles

canyons, however. After the long, hot desert summer, the river may shrink back to its usual width and much of the mud will dry, once again allowing easier access under the trestle.

If you elect to take this trip, plan to camp in the BLM campground on the east side of Afton Canyon Road. This campground is closest to the collecting site and affords covered picnic tables, an outhouse, barbecues, and numerous RV and tent camping sites. Bring ample water, as this is a dry camp. At the time of my visit there was a minimal charge per night, with a Golden Age discount.

The geology of the area is varied and interesting. The canyons of the collecting area are composed of compacted mud and sand that have been carved into fanciful spires and minarets through erosion. Be sure to take your camera into the canyon to capture the interesting natural formations.

Abundant collecting material is found in the main canyon, but hiking the narrow side cuts yields more varied and abundant material.

The material at this site consists of red and yellow jasper, agate, opalite in pastel shades of pink and pistachio green, and occasional calcite rhombs. I also found half a nodule filled with finger-size quartz crystals but could find no more. Plan to visit the other two canyons; some rockhounds claim these for their favorite collecting areas.

A barite deposit is reported to be somewhere in the area, but I have yet to locate it. Hematite is also supposed to be found in the canyon right behind the campground, although no other collectibles have been found there. Besides your camera, take a lunch or snack and drinking water. The hike to the canyon is not a long one, but the canyon and its narrow side ravines are so interesting that you may wander for hours just looking and exploring. One day I spent a lovely day collecting with two other rockhounds I met at the Afton Campground. Irene was piloting her camper solo, and Hal, another RVer, was an avid rockhound. The view from the top of the canyon is spectacular.

Turquoise at Old Toltec Mine

Land type: Desert hills
Elevation: 4,400 feet
Best season: October to April
Land manager: BLM
Material: Turquoise
Tools: Rock pick, collecting bag, chisel, rake, shovel, screen
Vehicle type: High-clearance two-wheel drive or four-wheel drive
Special attractions: None
Maps: USGS Turquoise Mountain
Lore: Turquoise is the sacred stone of Native Americans because of its protective and healing qualities.
Finding the site: Take I-15 from Baker heading east and exit at Halloran Springs. Drive north, veering right at Francis Springs Road, for a total of 7.3 miles. Keep to the left and drive up toward the radio tower. Do not go up to the tower, but continue on the southwest road for 1.2 miles. (Ignore the road to your right.) Drive an additional 1.1 miles on the southwest road, then turn right (northwest) and drive 0.2 mile. Stop here and walk northwest 0.5 mile to the mine. If you have a 4x4, you may wish to attempt the road to the mine, following the mileages on the map.

Rockhounding

This is the only turquoise collecting site I know of in California that is available to the public. The pieces are generally small and would be most suitable for "channel-work" jewelry. Use a rake or garden cultivator to dig through the tailings piles. A shovel would be useful for digging deeper into the tailings to access the sky-blue material overlooked by previous collectors. A fine-mesh screen, 0.25 inch, would also be useful in screening out turquoise pieces.

The old tunnel workings are unsafe to enter, so confine your collecting to tailings piles, gullies, and washes.

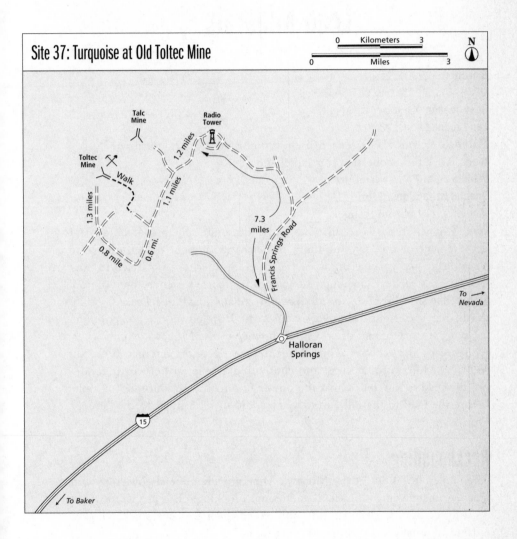

Site 37: Turquoise at Old Toltec Mine

0 Kilometers 3
0 Miles 3

N

Talc
Mine

Radio
Tower

Toltec
Mine

Walk

1.2 miles

1.1 miles

1.3 miles

0.8 mile

0.6 mi.

7.3
miles

Francis Springs Road

To →
Nevada

Halloran
Springs

15

↙ To Baker

Clark Mountain Copper and Lead Minerals

Land type: Desert hills
Elevation: 3,900 feet
GPS: N35 30.23' / W115 36.08'
Best season: October to April
Land manager: BLM
Material: Azurite, chrysocolla, malachite, smithsonite, galena, sphalerite
Tools: Rock pick, collecting bag, chisel, shovel
Vehicle type: Four-wheel drive
Special attractions: None
Maps: USGS Mescal Range
Lore: Copper minerals of all types and smithsonite aid in meditation and development of the "psychic body." Galena was thought to "ground" one emotionally and balance the body functions. Sphalerite was carried to protect against treachery, enabling its owner to recognize treachery by intuition.
Finding the site: Take I-15 from Baker and exit at Cima Road. Drive 0.7 mile north, then turn right and drive 4.1 miles east. Turn left (north) and continue 0.7 mile. Turn right and drive a short distance to the Mohawk Mine.

To reach the Copper World Mine, return the short distance from the Mohawk Mine, turning right and continuing 1 mile farther north, ignoring the road to the left. Cross the power line road and continue 0.7 mile. Ignore the road to the left and drive an additional 1.5 miles to the Copper World Mine.

Rockhounding

The numerous dumps of the Mohawk Mine provide mineral collectors with nice metallic specimens of galena and resinous-looking sphalerite. Keep an eye open for occasional specimens of smithsonite, which crystallizes in the botryoidal form usually as a coating on other rocks.

The Copper World Mine is a great spot for collecting fine specimens of the copper minerals azurite, malachite, and chrysocolla. My friend Herman once found a fabulous palm-size piece of chrysocolla there.

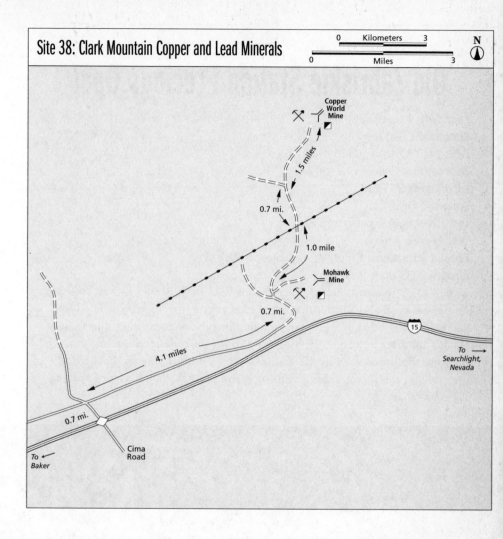

The Copper World Mine was open to rockhounds on my last visit, but it does go through spates of reopening for production, which closes it to rockhound access every time new gem material is discovered. When the vein of new gem material pinches out, the mine is then shut down and again made available for rockhounding.

Old Zabriskie Station Precious Opal

Land type: Desert hills
Elevation: 1,300 feet
GPS: N35 53.18' / W116 10.88'
Best season: October to April
Land manager: BLM
Material: Opal
Tools: Rock pick, collecting bag
Vehicle type: Any
Special attractions: Death Valley National Park
Maps: USGS Ibex Pass
Lore: Today's superstitions consider opal a "bad luck" stone, and supposedly only those born in October may wear it. However, the ancients revered opal and believed it aided its wearer in attaining invisibility and astral projection.
Finding the site: From CA 127 south of Death Valley Junction, take the road opposite the ruins of Zabriskie Station west 0.2 mile. Hunt the opal by digging among the hills and mud cliffs or going through the tailings of digging done by others.

Clay concretion with precious opal. PHOTO SHEP KOSS

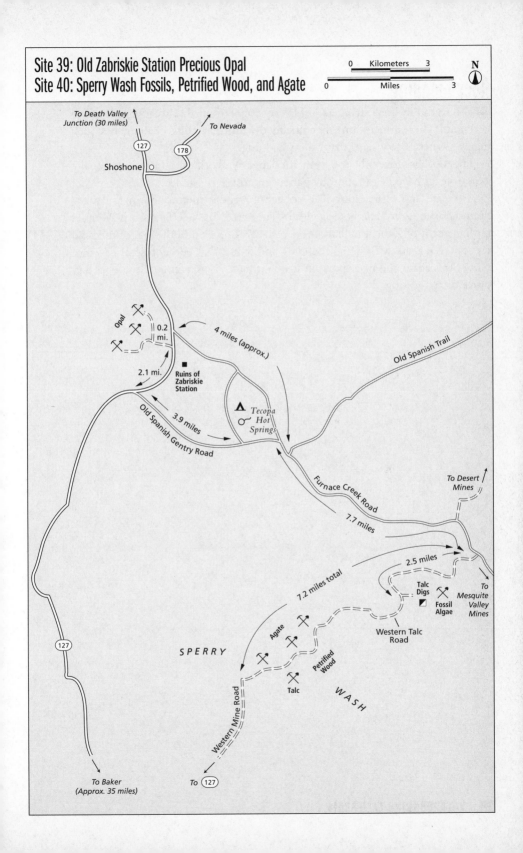

Site 39: Old Zabriskie Station Precious Opal
Site 40: Sperry Wash Fossils, Petrified Wood, and Agate

0   Kilometers   3

0   Miles   3

N

To Death Valley
Junction (30 miles)

To Nevada

127

178

Shoshone

Opal

0.2
mi.

4 miles (approx.)

Old Spanish Trail

2.1 mi.

Ruins of
Zabriskie
Station

3.9 miles

Tecopa
Hot
Springs

Old Spanish Gentry Road

Furnace Creek Road

To Desert
Mines

7.7 miles

2.5 miles

127

7.2 miles total

Talc
Digs

Fossil
Algae

To
Mesquite
Valley
Mines

SPERRY

Agate

Western Talc
Road

Petrified
Wood

WASH

Talc

Western Mine Road

To Baker
(Approx. 35 miles)

To 127

Rockhounding

Opal is found in small stringers inside clay concretions that weather out of the mud cliffs. These concretions are embedded within the cliffs. I had my best luck digging where I saw signs that others had dug.

The opal is generally too thin for lapidary work, although occasionally larger pieces have been found by patient hunting.

An agate and chalcedony rose collecting spot is mentioned in the rockhound classic *Gem Trails of California* by James R. Mitchell. This site is 24 miles farther north of Zabriskie Station on CA 127. Look on both sides of the road for scattered agate with orange banding and white chalcedony roses. I have not visited this agate and rose spot, but it might be a thought should the opal digs prove disappointing.

Sperry Wash Fossils, Petrified Wood, and Agate

(See map on page 119.)

Land type: Desert
Elevation: 1,750 feet
GPS: N35 46.13' / W116 10.88'
Best season: October to April
Land manager: BLM
Material: Fossils, petrified wood, agate
Tools: Rock pick, collecting bag, chisel
Vehicle type: Four-wheel drive
Special attractions: Tecopa Hot Springs
Maps: USGS Tecopa and Tecopa Dunes
Lore: Fossils and petrified wood were believed to ensure long life to their owners. Agate brought strength and courage and was worn in battle.
Finding the site: From CA 127 near the ruins of Zabriskie Station, turn east onto Furnace Creek Road. Drive approximately 4 miles southeast. Stay on Furnace Creek Road where it branches right, away from the Old Spanish Trail Road. Drive an additional 7.7 miles and turn right onto Western Talc Road. Drive 2.5 miles and turn left, heading to the talc mine. Here you can collect talc specimens and fossil algae.

Back out on Western Talc Road, go another 4.7 miles. Between the talc mine and this point, agate and petrified wood may be gathered on both sides of the road.

This area is now in a designated Wilderness Area, but if you take Furnace Creek Road to the old Western Mine Road (Sperry Wash), BLM is still keeping this route open to the collecting area. However, be aware that 30 feet to either side of this wash is closed to all mechanized vehicles (meaning no wagons, bicycles, etc.).

Rockhounding

This site has long been a favorite of rockhounds. The fossils are located to the east of the talc pit in the limestone cliffs. The petrified wood and agate are still fairly plentiful, even after decades of collecting.

Be safety-conscious at all times. Don't feed any rockhounds to the buzzards.
Photo by Garret Romaine

Although the talc mine is currently inoperative, it is advisable to respect all No Trespassing signs.

Tecopa Hot Springs is a spot to camp and relax after a rockhound trip. There are several RV campgrounds in the area where you can soak away aches and pains in the mineral-rich waters.

Gem Hill Agate, Rhyolite, and Common Opal

Land type: Desert hills
Elevation: 2,800 feet
GPS: N34 55.400' / W118 10.614'
Best season: October to May
Land manager: BLM
Material: Agate, rhyolite, common opal
Tools: Rock pick, collecting bag, shovel
Vehicle type: Any
Special attractions: Tropico Gold Mine tour

Gem Hill green opal and agate cabachon. PHOTO BY SHEP KOSS

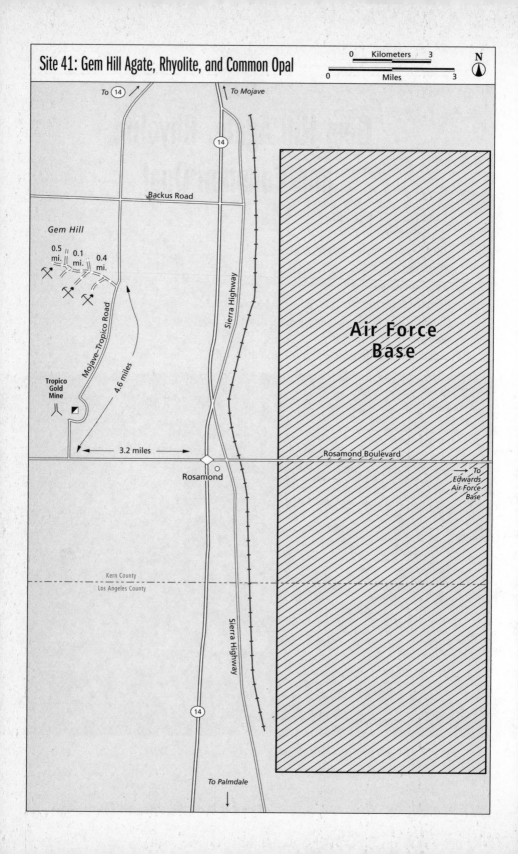

Site 41: Gem Hill Agate, Rhyolite, and Common Opal

Kilometers
0   3

Miles
0   3

N

To (14)

To Mojave

(14)

Backus Road

Gem Hill

0.5 mi.   0.1 mi.   0.4 mi.

Mojave-Tropico Road

4.6 miles

Tropico Gold Mine

Sierra Highway

Air Force Base

3.2 miles

Rosamond Boulevard

Rosamond

To Edwards Air Force Base

Kern County
Los Angeles County

Sierra Highway

(14)

To Palmdale

Maps: USGS Soledad Mountain

Lore: Agate brings courage and strength. Rhyolite is the stone of "self-realization," and common opal was thought to enhance wealth and relationships by increasing one's self-esteem.

Finding the site: Exit CA 14 at Rosamond Boulevard in Rosamond and head west 3.2 miles to Mojave-Tropico Road. Turn right (north) and drive 4.6 miles; turn left. Just about any spot to the right or left of the road from where it turns off Mojave-Tropico Road is a good place to find agate. Or follow the mileages indicated on the map.

Rockhounding

This has always been one of my favorite sites for collecting agate. The agate occurs in a variety of colors and patterns, as does the rhyolite. Near the Tropico Gold Mine, much of the rhyolite contains clear quartz crystals. The petrified wood occurs in green and white, and most of the common opal found here is green or white.

Look on the flats and hills adjacent to the road, and dig into the greenish deposits.

San Gabriel River Gold

Land type: Inland mountains
Elevation: 7,000 feet
Best season: Year-round
Land manager: USDAFS
Material: Gold
Tools: Gold pan, sluice box, shovel, pick, buckets
Vehicle type: Any
Special attractions: Follow's Camp Mining Museum
Maps: USGS Glendora
For more information: USDA Forest Service; (818) 335-1251
Accommodations: Tent and RV camping available at Camp Williams (818-910-1126) and Follow's Camp (818-910-1100)
Lore: Gold symbolizes wealth and wisdom and is used to alleviate arthritis pain.
Finding the site: From I-210 take the Azusa Boulevard off-ramp (CA 39) and drive north toward the mountains for 2.8 miles. Drive up into the mountains for 8.9 miles to East Fork Road. Turn right onto East Fork Road, which crosses the San Gabriel River below. Continue another 4 miles to Camp Williams Restaurant and campground. You may prospect for gold anywhere from Camp Williams to the end of the road at Heaton Flat.

Rockhounding

Flakes of gold and an occasional nugget may be found along the banks of the San Gabriel River between the Camp Williams Restaurant and Heaton Flat at the end of the road. Panning and sluicing are allowed along the river. Motorized equipment, such as suction dredges and highbankers, require permits and are subject to restrictions. It is best to call the forest service for current regulations concerning motorized equipment.

Knowledge of how to use a gold pan and sluice box is helpful. While gold is found along the river all season long, gold will be more abundant after a heavy rainfall.

Look for concentrations of gold on the downstream sides of large rocks and boulders, among tree roots at the water's edge, and at the inside curves or bends in the river, sandbars, and where water flow is slowed.

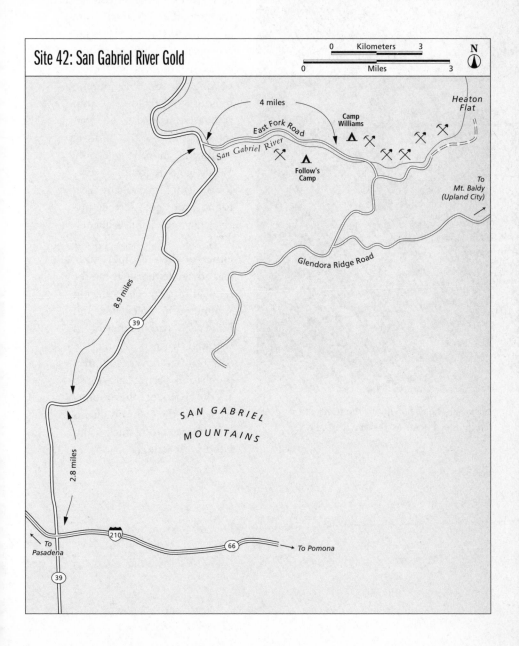

Kilometers

0   3

Miles

0   3

N

Heaton
Flat

4 miles

East Fork Road

Camp
Williams

San Gabriel River

Follow's
Camp

To
Mt. Baldy
(Upland City)

Glendora Ridge Road

8.9 miles

39

SAN GABRIEL

MOUNTAINS

2.8 miles

210

66

To
Pasadena

To Pomona

39

Spending a day playing in the water can be great family fun. PHOTO BY GARRET ROMAINE

You may prospect for gold at Follow's Camp if you are camping there. A small store at Follow's Camp sells some prospecting equipment and occasionally offers gold prospecting classes. The mining museum at Follow's Camp is interesting to see and has information on the historic southern California gold rush. While gold is found at Follow's Camp, I personally have found more gold farther upriver beyond Camp Williams.

If you wish to camp at either of these campgrounds, it is advisable to call ahead for reservations, especially during summer. On weekends and holidays a parking permit is required to park along the San Gabriel River. You may purchase a permit at a kiosk at the base of the mountains or at the Camp Williams Restaurant. Good luck—and good prospecting!

Wrightwood Actinolite

Land type: Alpine forest
Elevation: 7,000 feet
Best season: March to October
Land manager: USDAFS
Material: Actinolite, actinolite crystals
Tools: Rock pick, collecting bag
Vehicle type: Any
Special attractions: None
Maps: USGS Big Pines, Mescal Creek, Mount San Antonio, and Telegraph Peak
Lore: Actinolite was believed to bring joy, luck, and wisdom.
Finding the site: From I-15 take CA 138 north to CA 2 and head west. Drive approximately 4 miles on CA 2 to the town of Wrightwood. Continue another 4 miles and turn left, remaining on CA 2 where CR N4 forks to the right. Continue another 6 miles. Park and search the washes and gullies on both sides of the road.

Another location for actinolite is reached by turning southeast onto Lone Pine Canyon Road in Wrightwood. Continue 0.5 mile to the big wash near the road. Most washes and gullies in this area will yield bright, silvery green–bladed actinolite as well as dense jade-green crystals.

Rockhounding

This is a good trip to take when desert temperatures reach their unbearable summertime highs. The more massive form of actinolite, which is rather soft and composed of interlocking bladed crystals, makes a nice addition to a mineral collection and a nice display piece because of its silvery green coloration. The monoclinic prismatic crystals are hard enough for jewelry making. I've had good luck finding the crystals at the Lone Pine Canyon Road location.

This is a nice place to bring a picnic lunch. The nearby town of Wrightwood also has a couple of good pizza parlors.

Wrightwood actinolite and rhodonite cab. PHOTO BY SHEP KOSS

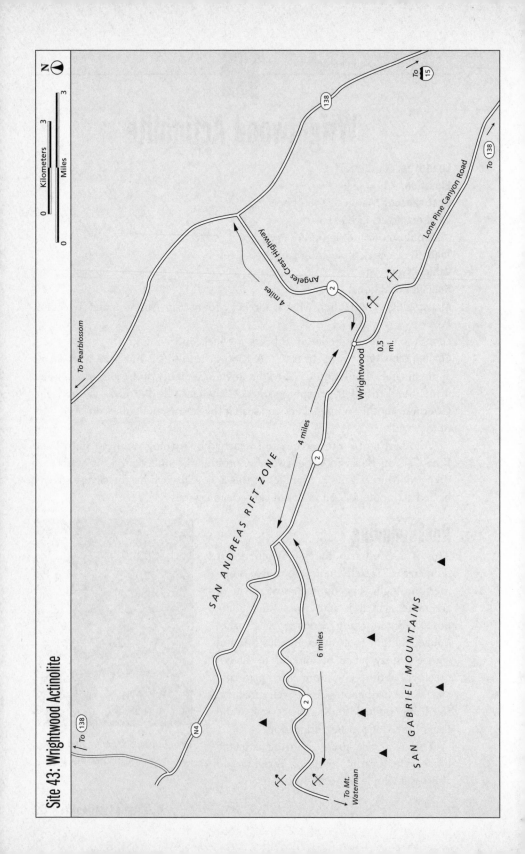

Site 43: Wrightwood Actinolite

In-Ko-Pah Park Asterated Quartz and Moonstone Feldspar

Land type: Desert hills
Elevation: 1,640 feet
GPS: N32 39.10' / W116 07.09'
Best season: September to May
Land manager: BLM and private property
Material: Asterated quartz, moonstone feldspar, garnet
Tools: Collecting bag, pick
Vehicle type: Any
Special attractions: None
Maps: USGS In-Ko-Pah Gorge
For more information: BLM Desert Access Guide McCain Valley #19
Lore: Quartz showing inner rainbows brought hope and inspiration. Feldspar was believed to have protective qualities. In the thirteenth century garnet was worn for strength, for protection, and to repel insects.
Finding the site: The amount of private property in this area is increasing. Be sure to gain permission before crossing any private property.

From I-8 take In-Ko-Pah Park Road, west-northwest of the highway. Drive several hundred yards to the road's end and park. Several trails head west to the nearby hills. An easy walk west will bring you to the moonstone feldspar site. Follow the float up the rocky hill to its source. Beware of a vertical shaft farther up the hill. To reach the asterated quartz site, follow the trail from In-Ko-Pah Park Road northwest to a low hill. The quartz litters the ground at the base of the hill. Occasional garnets can be found in matrix at the quartz site.

Rockhounding

When cut along one axis, asterated quartz, also called cat's-eye quartz, reveals asterism, a star-shaped optical phenomenon. Look for pieces that display flashes of rainbow color. This seems to be the best clue as to which pieces will display asterism when cut. Experimentation in cutting will be required to discover which axis displays the phenomenon, and care will be required in grinding to preserve asteration.

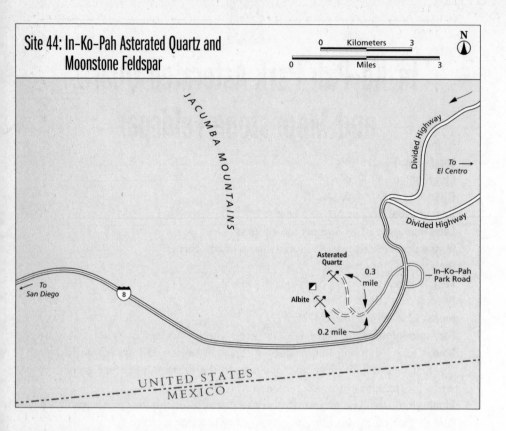

The seed- to pea-size garnets found at this location are not gem quality, but they make nice specimen pieces when removed with matrix.

Moonstone feldspar, or albite, is a variety of plagioclase feldspar. Opalescence becomes pronounced when the albite is cut and polished. Again, experimentation in cutting will determine which cleavage axis most demonstrates the desired luster. The albite at this location was mined in years past for use in pottery and china production. This location is about 3 miles from the US-Mexico border.

Coyote Mountains Fossils and More

Land type: Desert hills
Elevation: 439 feet
GPS: N32 48.42' / W115 57.94'
Best season: October to May
Land manager: BLM
Material: Fossils, mica "books," black tourmaline

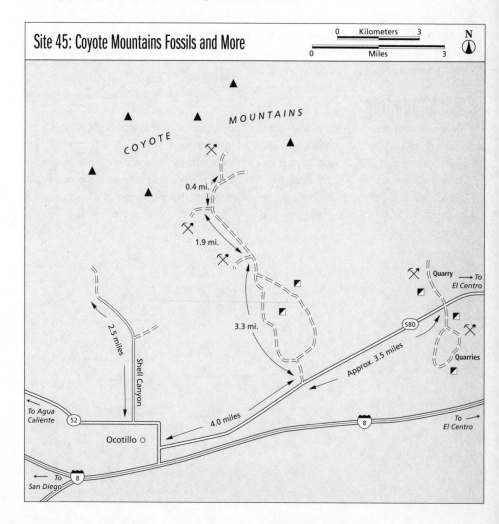

Site 45: Coyote Mountains Fossils and More

Vehicle type: Any

Tools: Rock pick, collecting bag

Special attractions: None

Maps: USGS Ocotillo and Painted Gorge

Lore: Fossils guaranteed a long life. Mica was believed to protect against earthquakes—good news for us Californians! Black tourmaline, or schorl, was thought to deflect black magic.

Finding the site: Take the Ocotillo exit off I-8 and head 4 miles east on CA S80. Turn left (north) onto Painted Gorge Road. The first collecting site is 3.3 miles up Painted Gorge Road and about 300 feet to the west of the road.

Driving 1.9 miles farther north on Painted Gorge Road, you will come to another collecting area, but you will need a 4x4 to negotiate this road. An additional site is located in another 0.4 mile. Turn north onto a road and park at the base of the hill. Walk up the hill and about 0.2 mile to the base of some more hills.

Rockhounding

Numerous types of fossil crustaceans may be collected at this site. Also, around the gravel pits one can collect samples of muscovite and biotite mica, some with numerous sheets making up tiny "books." Black tourmaline, or schorl, may also be collected here, along with occasional pink and lavender pieces of lepidolite. You may also find calcite and calcite crystals on or around the gravel pits. There are a couple campgrounds in the area where you can pitch your tent or park your RV.

Patrick's Point Beach Agates

Land type: Coastal
Elevation: 180 feet
GPS: N41 08.56' / W124 09.56'
Best season: September to May
Land manager: California Department of Parks and Recreation
Material: Beach-washed agate
Tools: Collecting bag
Vehicle type: Any
Special attractions: Beach recreation and camping
Maps: USGS Trinidad

Most black sands contain traces of gold, platinum, and other rare earth elements.
PHOTO BY GARRET ROMAINE

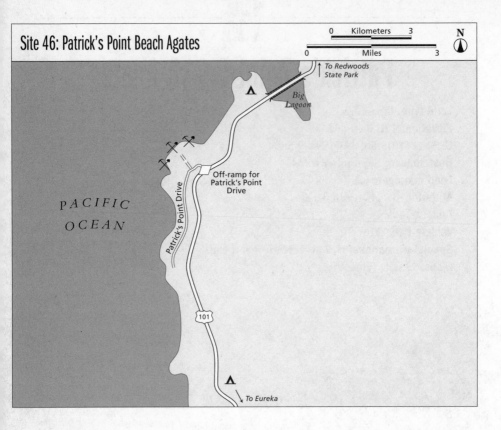

0   Kilometers   3

N

0   Miles   3

To Redwoods
State Park

Big
Lagoon

Off-ramp for
Patrick's Point
Drive

Patrick's Point Drive

PACIFIC

OCEAN

101

To Eureka

Lore: Agate was believed to protect its wearer from harm, both physical and occult, as well as bring courage in battle.

Finding the site: From US 101 north of Eureka, take the Patrick's Point exit and head west about 0.5 mile to the beach at Patrick's Point State Park.

Rockhounding

This site yields beach-washed agate. When I was there last, there were restrictions on how much agate could be collected. Check with rangers for changes in restrictions before collecting. Camping is available at the state park.

Low tide during winter is the best time to collect, as well as after winter storms.

Agate Beach Jasper, Agate, and Petrified Wood

Land type: Coastal
Elevation: 250 feet
GPS: N37 53.83' / W122 42.65'
Best season: September to April
Land manager: California Department of Parks and Recreation
Material: Oil agate, jasper, petrified wood

Look for petrified wood at the beach, in desert dry washes, along rivers, and in just about any gravel accumulation. PHOTO BY GARRET ROMAINE

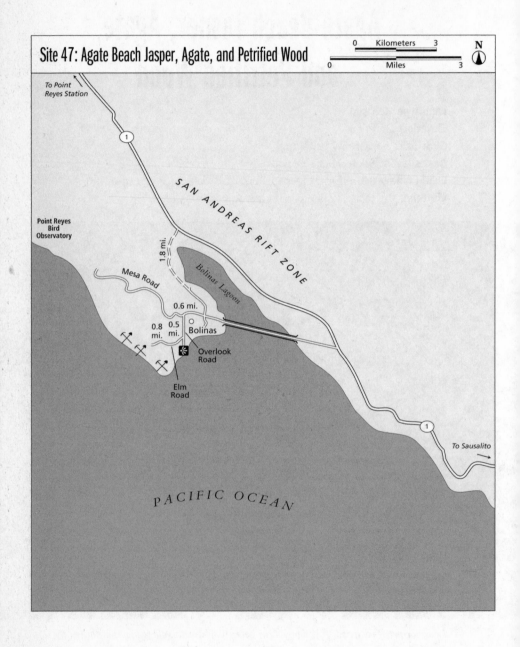

Site 47: Agate Beach Jasper, Agate, and Petrified Wood

Kilometers

Miles

N

To Point
Reyes Station

1

SAN ANDREAS RIFT ZONE

Point Reyes
Bird
Observatory

1.8 mi.

Mesa Road

Bolinas Lagoon

0.6 mi.

0.8
mi.

0.5
mi.

Bolinas

Overlook
Road

Elm
Road

1

To Sausalito

PACIFIC OCEAN

Tools: Collecting bag
Vehicle type: Any
Special attractions: Point Reyes Bird Observatory natural history tours
Maps: USGS Bolinas
Lore: Agate and jasper were believed to bring protection and courage. Jasper was used in rituals to bring rain. Ownership of agatized petrified wood would gain all the attributes of agate plus help ensure long life, much the same as a fossil. Some believed that petrified wood protected against drowning—a good thing to have when beach collecting.
Finding the site: Exit CA 1 at Bolinas Road and head southwest 1.8 miles to Mesa Road. Turn right onto Mesa Road and drive 0.6 mile to Overlook Road. Turn left; drive 0.5 mile to Elm Road and turn right. Drive 0.8 mile on Elm Road to the beach.

Rockhounding

The prize to be found here is "oil agate"—a clear to translucent agate with dark spots. You may also find occasional pieces of petrified whalebone, as well as abalone shell. Abalone shell can be tumble polished and used in lapidary projects. As with all beach collecting, check with rangers on restrictions.

As with most coastal sites, after winter storms is the best time to collect.

Beach-Washed Jade and Actinolite at Jade Cove

Land type: Coastal
Elevation: 400 feet
GPS: N35 54.82' / W121 28.10'
Best season: October to March
Land manager: California Department of Parks and Recreation
Material: Jade, actinolite
Tools: Collecting bag
Vehicle type: Any
Special attractions: Hearst Castle near San Simeon
Maps: USGS Cape San Martin
Lore: Jade was thought to bring prosperity, luck, and wisdom to its wearer. Actinolite was thought to have similar attributes to jade, although somewhat milder. It was also believed to assist in ridding oneself of unwanted conditions.
Finding the site: Exit CA 1 to any of the beach locations between the town of Gorda and Plaskett Creek. All this stretch is Jade Beach.

Large Jade Cove water-polished jade. PHOTO BY SHEP KOSS

Classic "slickensides" feature is evidence of faulting. PHOTO BY GARRET ROMAINE

Use caution when climbing down the steep cliffs to the Pacific Ocean beaches. PHOTO BY GARRET ROMAINE

Rockhounding

This site has long been known for its beach-washed jade pebbles and boulders. This site was recently removed from collecting status. However, due to efforts by several rock clubs, the restrictions have lessened slightly and the site is expected to be returned to collecting status soon. Should you decide to visit this site, be sure to obey any signs either prohibiting jade collecting or listing a change in restrictions.

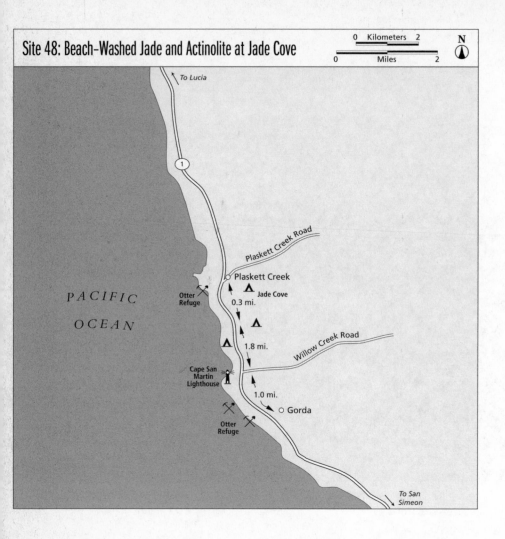

0   Kilometers   2

0   Miles   2

N

To Lucia

1

Plaskett Creek Road

PACIFIC

OCEAN

Otter
Refuge

Plaskett Creek

Jade Cove

0.3 mi.

Willow Creek Road

1.8 mi.

Cape San
Martin
Lighthouse

1.0 mi.

Gorda

Otter
Refuge

To San
Simeon

The best time to collect here is at low tide during winter, especially after storms. When you collect at low tide, keep an eye on the water line. Some areas of this beach may be cut off from escape when the tide comes in. If you are taking children, watch that they do not become trapped by the incoming tide.

Moonstone Beach

Land type: Coastal
Elevation: 500 feet
GPS: N35 33.98' / W121 06.52'
Best season: November to March
Land manager: California Department of Parks and Recreation
Material: Moonstones
Tools: Collecting bag
Vehicle type: Any
Special attractions: The town of Cambria and nearby Hearst Castle
Maps: USGS San Simeon, Pico Creek, and Cambria
Accommodations: Camping available at two state parks off CA 1 just north of Cambria

Large, raw chunk of feldspar, before tumbling and turning into "moonstone." PHOTO BY GARRET ROMAINE

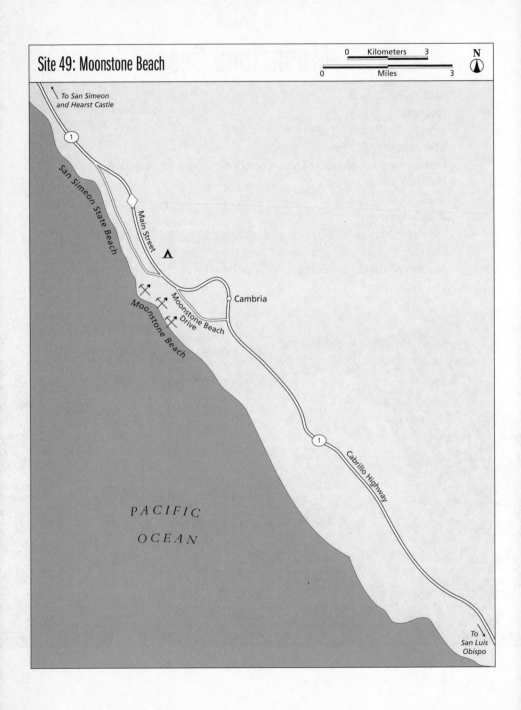

Site 49: Moonstone Beach

0 Kilometers 3

0 Miles 3

N

To San Simeon
and Hearst Castle

1

San Simeon State Beach

Main Street

Moonstone Beach Drive

Cambria

Moonstone Beach

1

Cabrillo Highway

PACIFIC

OCEAN

To
San Luis
Obispo

Lore: Moonstones have long been associated with witchcraft and goddess worship. They were believed to protect their wearer against malefic magic and enhance prophetic dreaming and psychic awareness.

Finding the site: From CA 1 in Cambria take Main Street to Moonstone Beach Drive. Moonstone Beach stretches from San Simeon to the town of Cambria.

Rockhounding

This site has long been famous for its beach-washed moonstones. Moonstone is a type of opalescent feldspar.

Cambria is a small town with numerous artists and artisans selling their wares in small, expensive shops. Hearst Castle was one of several magnificent homes built by publishing magnate William Randolph Hearst. Tours are available by reservation.

Jalama Beach Agate and Marcasite

Land type: Coastal
Elevation: 850 feet
GPS: N34 30.66' / W120 30.06'
Best season: September to March
Land manager: Santa Barbara County
Material: Agate, fossils, marcasite
Tools: Rock pick, collecting bag, chisels
Vehicle type: Any
Special attractions: Jalama Beach camping and beachcombing
Maps: USGS Lompoc Hills
Accommodations: Camping available at the state campground
Lore: Agate was thought to bring its wearer protection and courage. Fossils ensured of long life. According to New Age sources, marcasite assists in dealing with and healing codependency issues.
Finding the site: Coming from Lompoc on CA 1, turn right onto Jalama Road at a sign indicating Jalama Beach. Be watchful; the small sign is easily missed. If you are coming from Buellton, you will make a left turn onto Jalama Road. Head toward the coast through hilly cattle country for 12 miles until you see the beach.

Rockhounding

This is a fantastic site for either tent or RV camping. You may camp on the beach or high on the cliff above, where the view is fabulous. Cement pads are provided for RV beach camping; there are no hookups. Bring your own drinking water, as the water sources at the beach are not suitable for drinking.

You can find tide pools here, and the beachcombing is great. Because this is a county beach, absolutely no collecting is permitted without a permit. Permits for collecting must be obtained through Santa Barbara County. Contact Sherman Hansen, SBCP Mid County Operations Manager, at jrauch@sbparks.org or (805) 686–5076.

From surf to mean high tide level is governed by the California Coastal Commission, which allows collecting within these boundaries. Translucent root beer–brown agate with white veining is plentiful.

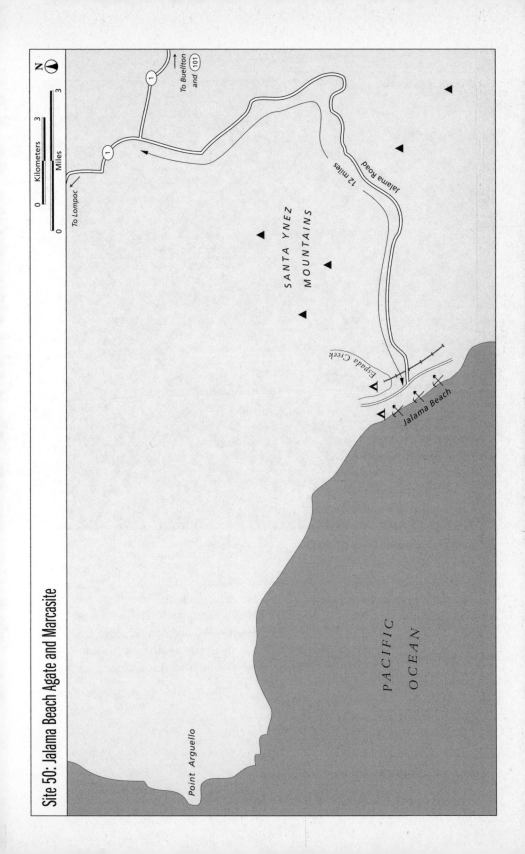

Site 50: Jalama Beach Agate and Marcasite

N

Kilometers
0   3

Miles
0   3

To Lompoc

To Buellton
and 101

Jalama Road

12 miles

SANTA YNEZ
MOUNTAINS

Espada Creek

Jalama Beach

PACIFIC
OCEAN

Point Arguello

Large mammal skeleton in the flotsam and jetsam. PHOTO BY GARRET ROMAINE

The beach was once the site of a Chumash Indian village. The village existed for centuries near the creek that runs down out of the hills and across the beach into the sea. The village was deserted when the Spanish invaders removed the Indians from their homes and took them to La Purisima Mission. The best time to collect here is off-season, when winter storms and the lack of vacationers ensure plentiful collecting material.

Gaviota Beach Minerals

Land type: Coastal
Elevation: 400 feet
GPS: N34 28.26' / W120 13.66'
Best season: October to March
Land manager: California Department of Parks and Recreation
Material: Minerals and plant fossils
Tools: Rock pick, collecting bag, chisel
Vehicle type: Any
Special attractions: Beach camping
Maps: USGS Gaviota
Accommodations: Camping available at the state campground
Lore: The ancients believed that possession of a fossil ensured long life.
Finding the site: From US 101 take the Gaviota Beach turnoff to Gaviota Beach.

Dogs are great companions for rockhounding adventures. PHOTO BY GARRET ROMAINE

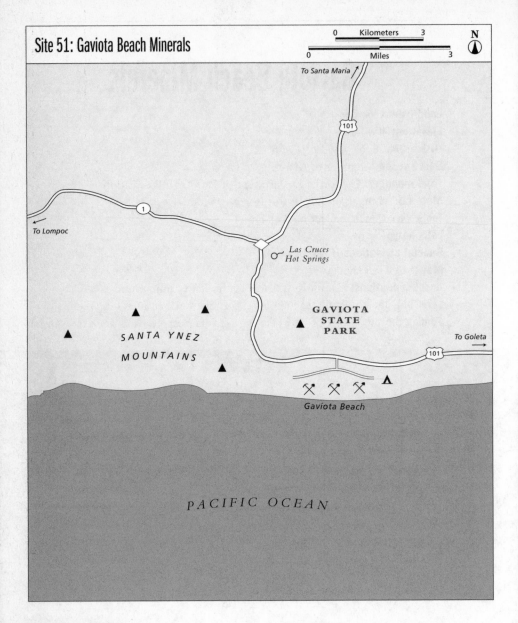

0   Kilometers   3

0   Miles   3

N

To Santa Maria

101

To Lompoc

1

Las Cruces
Hot Springs

SANTA YNEZ
MOUNTAINS

GAVIOTA
STATE
PARK

To Goleta

101

Gaviota Beach

PACIFIC OCEAN

Rockhounding

This site offers a variety of fossils; however, vertebrate fossil collecting is forbidden under federal antiquities laws. Minerals and rocks to be collected here include agate, jasper, and chert. The best time for collecting is during the winter months. Beach-washed material is much more plentiful after winter storms.

Southern Coast Beachcombing

Land type: Coastal
Elevation: 340 feet
Best season: December to February
Land manager: Los Angeles County
Material: Beach agate, jasper
Tools: Collecting bag
Vehicle type: Any
Special attractions: Beach recreation and people watching
Maps: USGS Redondo Beach and Venice Beach
Lore: Agate and jasper purportedly bring courage and protection to their owners. Jasper is valued by Native Americans for rain-bringing properties.
Finding the site: From I-405 take Torrance Boulevard west to Redondo Beach or El Segundo Boulevard west to El Segundo Beach. The Pacific Coast Highway (CA 1) runs many miles north and south along the coast. Most roadways crossing the Pacific Coast Highway will take you west to any number of other beaches you may wish to visit.

Rockhounding

El Segundo and Hermosa Beaches are collected for their colorful ocean-tumbled agates. Redondo Beach not only has beach-washed agate but also "moonstones." The Redondo Beach moonstones are actually a translucent white agate.

These beach sites are within the busy urban sprawl of Los Angeles County. Therefore, the best and least crowded times to collect are after winter storms bring new material up onto the beach and during winter months, when cold, damp, and foggy weather keeps hordes of sunbathers at home. Check with rangers for collecting regulations but, as on all California beaches, the area from the surf to mean high tide line is managed by the California Coastal Commission, which allows casual collecting.

Most of the beaches provide barbecue pits for after-collecting picnics.

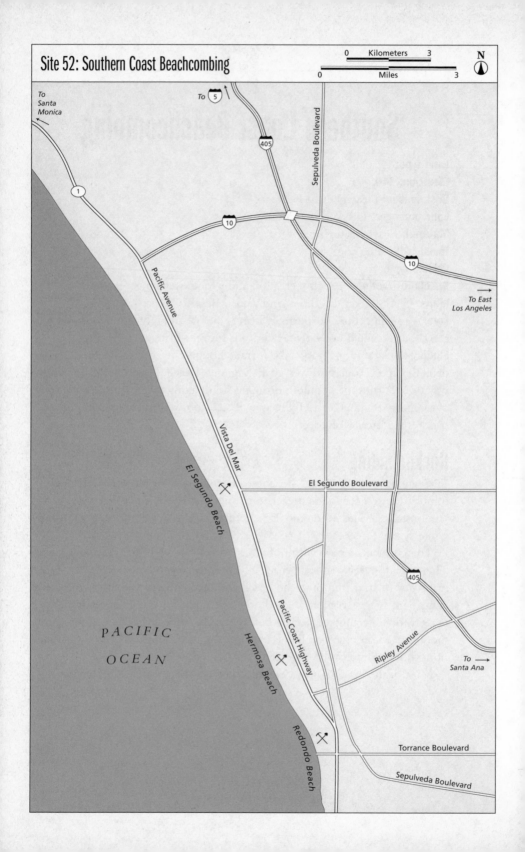

Palos Verdes Beach Barite Crystals

Land type: Coastal cliffs
Elevation: 600 feet
Best season: Year-round
Land manager: Los Angeles County
Material: Cockscomb barite crystals
Tools: Rock pick, collecting bag, chisel
Vehicle type: Any
Special attractions: Beach recreation
Maps: USGS San Pedro, Redondo Beach, and Torrance
Lore: According to New Age beliefs, barite assists one in knowing that all things are possible.

Palos Verdes cockscomb barite. PHOTO BY SHEP KOSS

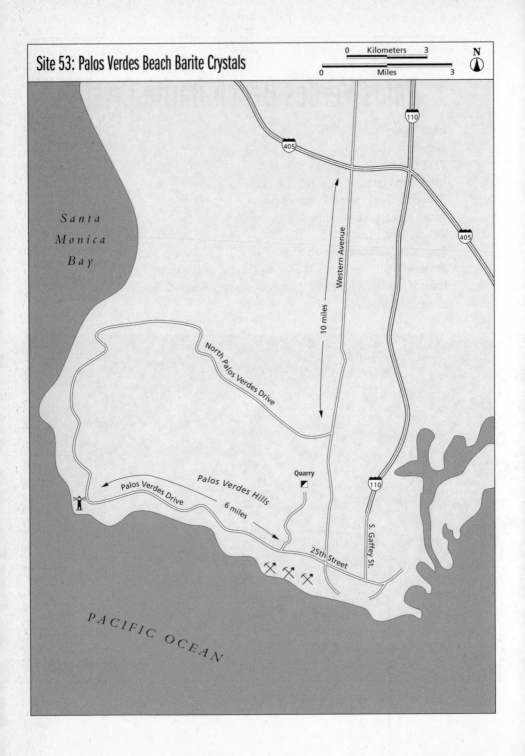

Site 53: Palos Verdes Beach Barite Crystals

Finding the site: Exit I-405 onto Western Avenue and head south approximately 10 miles. Turn right on 25th Street, which becomes Palos Verdes Drive from here to the lighthouse, approximately 6 miles. Park your vehicle and walk down to the beach on one of the numerous paths down the cliffs. Be careful when descending to the beach; some paths are steeper than others.

Rockhounding

At the bases of the beach cliffs below the quarry is the best area to collect barite-covered rocks, which erode out of the sea cliffs. The barite crystals are white to beige, generally translucent, and form in the cockscomb habit. They will generally fluoresce a cream color under an ultraviolet lamp. The best time to collect is during the winter months, when the beaches are basically deserted and winter storms have eroded out the cliff material.

Fossil shells may be found embedded in the cliffs between the lighthouse and Marineland. These collecting areas are also good for picnic lunches and enjoying the beach and people watching during warmer months.

Anderson Lake Agate and Jasper

Land type: Foothills
Elevation: 1,300 feet
Best season: April to October
Land manager: Santa Clara County
Material: Jasper, agate, magnesite
Tools: Rock pick, collecting bag
Vehicle type: Any
Special attractions: Rosicrucian Park in nearby San Jose
Maps: USGS Morgan Hill and Mount Sizer
Camping: Camping available at Henry W. Coe State Park, located about 12 miles northeast of Anderson Lake on East Dunne Avenue
Lore: Jasper and agate were worn for protection and courage, while jasper was used in Native American rainmaking ceremonies. Magnesite is used during meditation to enhance visualization.
Finding the site: As US 101 passes through the town of Morgan Hill, exit at either East Dunne Avenue or Cochran Avenue and head northeast 3 to 4 miles to Anderson Lake County Park. Colorful agate and jasper may be collected all along the lakeshore.

Kids often get distracted with lizards, frogs, and bugs. Encourage your children to bring home rocks, and leave the wildlife in the wild. PHOTO BY GARRET ROMAINE

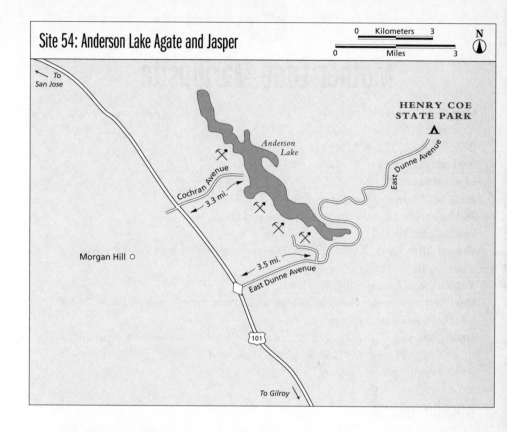

0   Kilometers   3

0   Miles   3

N

To San Jose

HENRY COE STATE PARK

Anderson Lake

East Dunne Avenue

Cochran Avenue

3.3 mi.

Morgan Hill

3.5 mi.

East Dunne Avenue

101

To Gilroy

Rockhounding

Since this is county property, park rangers have been known to prohibit rock collecting. Please check current status with rangers, since this has been an on-again, off-again policy over the years. Boating and fishing can also be enjoyed at this location.

On the south end of the reservoir, look for blue and white agate or some that is blue and clear. At the north end look for white magnesite with reddish brown veins. Jasper is found all around. This site was contributed by two friends of mine from San Jose, George Price and Sharon Frazier.

Of further interest in nearby San Jose is Rosicrucian Park at Naglee and Park Avenues off Alameda Boulevard. The park takes up 1 city block and is home to a planetarium offering daily shows; an Egyptian museum with authentic mummies and other Egyptian, Assyrian, and Babylonian artifacts; a gift shop; and an espresso bar.

Mother Lode Mariposite

Land type: Oak-covered hills
Elevation: 2,700 feet
GPS: N37 42.79' / W120 12.69'
Best season: April to October
Land manager: BLM
Material: Mariposite and serpentine
Tools: Rock pick, collecting bag, chisel, gad bar
Vehicle type: Any
Special attractions: The California Division of Mines and Geology Mineral Museum in Mariposa
Maps: USGS Coulterville
Lore: Serpentine was thought to protect its wearers from stinging insects and bites of venomous serpents.
Finding the site: The mariposite is located in a road cut just west of the junction of CA 49 and CA 132 at Coulterville and is clearly visible due to its vibrant bluish green coloring.

Rockhounding

Mariposite is a type of mica with a bit of chromium, which colors it a greenish blue. It is found in white quartz in the Coulterville area. The combination of greenish blue and white is striking. Mariposite makes fine display pieces, but

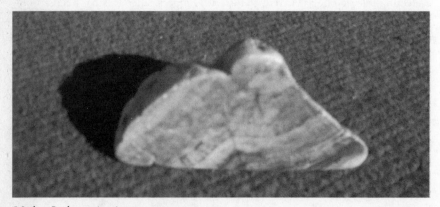

Mother Lode mariposite. PHOTO BY SHEP KOSS

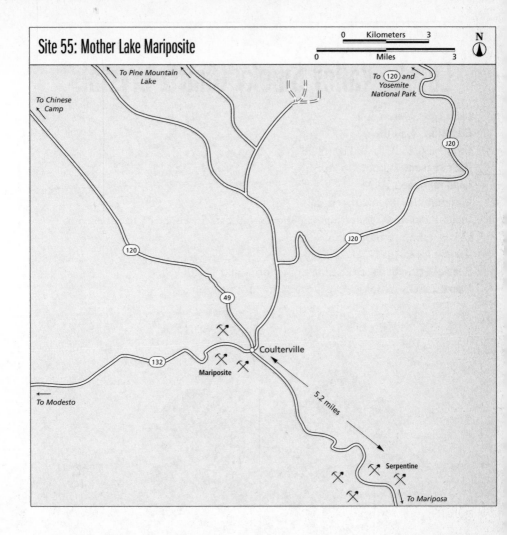

Kilometers

Miles

N

To Pine Mountain Lake

To Chinese Camp

To (120) and Yosemite National Park

J20

J20

120

49

Coulterville

132

Mariposite

To Modesto

5.2 miles

Serpentine

To Mariposa

it is usually too soft for lapidary work unless well integrated into the quartz. Serpentine can be found all along CA 49 in road cuts between Mariposa and Coulterville. The quality ranges from poor to good.

The CDMG Mineral Museum in Mariposa is a highly recommended stop. It is located about 15 miles southwest of Coulterville in Mariposa, right off CA 49 at the county fairground. The museum has one of the finest gem, mineral, and gold displays in California, as well as mining displays and a children's hands-on mineral collection.

Eureka Valley Smoky Quartz Crystals

Land type: Desert hills
Elevation: 4,500 feet
GPS: N36 55.35' / W118 09.28'
Best season: October to April
Land manager: BLM
Material: Smoky quartz crystals
Tools: Rock pick, collecting bag, shovel, gad bar, chisels, crack hammer, gloves, shovel, rake, eye protection
Vehicle type: Any
Special attractions: Bristlecone pine forest and Death Valley
Maps: USGS Crooked Creek and Chocolate Mountain

Always be considerate of cultural artifacts. Use your camera, not your rock hammer.
PHOTO BY GARRET ROMAINE

Site 56: Eureka Valley Smoky Quartz Crystals

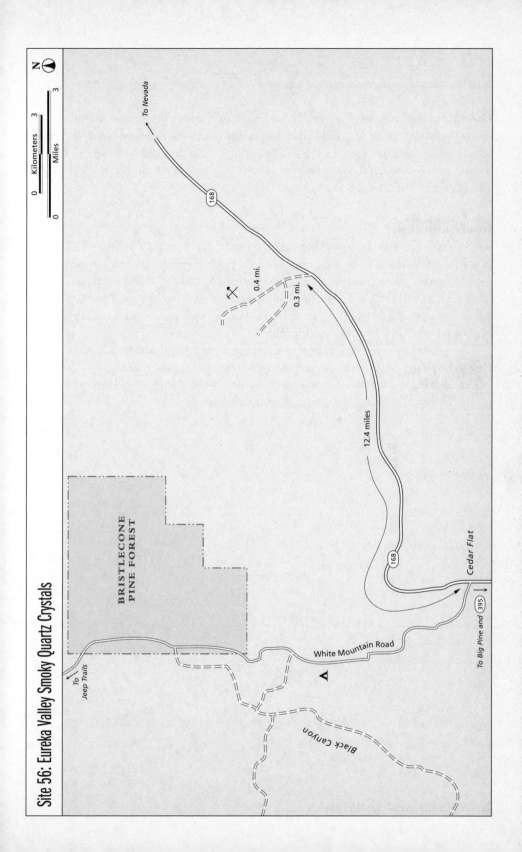

Lore: Smokey quartz was worn or carried to dispel negative energies, depression, or anger.

Finding the site: From Big Pine head 13.2 miles east then northeast on CA 168. At the junction of CA 168 and White Mountain Road, continue on CA 168 for 12.4 miles to a dirt road on the left. Take this road and go 0.3 mile, ignoring the road to the left. Drive another 0.4 mile to a low hill. Seams of smoky quartz crystals run through the hill.

Rockhounding

Smoky quartz crystals are found here in seams and pockets in the country rock of the low hill. You'll need gads, chisels, and a crack hammer. Gloves will be useful to protect your hands. A rake or hand cultivator will be helpful in raking loose crystals from the soil. Be careful in opening crystal pockets so as not to break the crystals. The color of these crystals varies from light to dark smoky gray or brown. They vary in size from tiny to several inches.

This is a remote site, so if you go here or plan to visit Death Valley National Park, take plenty of water and make sure someone knows you're going.

I've heard that more crystals and some fossils may be found in and around nearby Black Canyon, but I haven't yet located any there.

Peterson Mountain Quartz Crystals

Land type: Sage-covered hills
Elevation: 4,800 feet
Best season: May to October
Land manager: BLM
Material: Clear, milky, rainbow, scepter, amethyst quartz crystals
Tools: Rock pick, collecting bag, chisels, shovel, iron rake or hand cultivator
Vehicle type: Four-wheel drive or high-clearance truck
Special attractions: None
Maps: USGS Beckworth
Lore: Quartz crystals were and are prized for their healing properties. Amethyst crystals were believed to prevent intoxication (this is good news!), bring prophetic dreams, and prevent oversleeping (more good news for today's commuters). Crystals were used in shamanic healing and ritual, and all types were believed to increase and strengthen the aura, the energy field that surrounds the wearer.
Finding the site: From the junction of US 395 and CA 70, drive north 7.2 miles. Take the dirt road to the right. A barbed-wire gate must be opened then closed after driving through. Drive 1.7 miles, ignoring all roads to the right and always remaining on the most defined road. Just before reaching the site, the road forks. Take the right fork, which is less rough and rutted, although both forks lead to the site. The flat plateau where the road ends provides ample parking and turnaround room for several vehicles.

Keep in mind that US 395 is a divided highway. If you end up on the wrong side, there are several dirt tracks leading through the center median that are used by the California Highway Patrol. Slow down, making sure that no one is behind you before crossing the median, or continue several miles to a paved turnaround.

Rockhounding

This site has long been known for its lovely and plentiful quartz crystals. The crystals are found in seams in the rock near the parking area, on the slopes, and in the dry creekbed near the parking area, as well as on the back and south sides of the mountain that rises above the parking area.

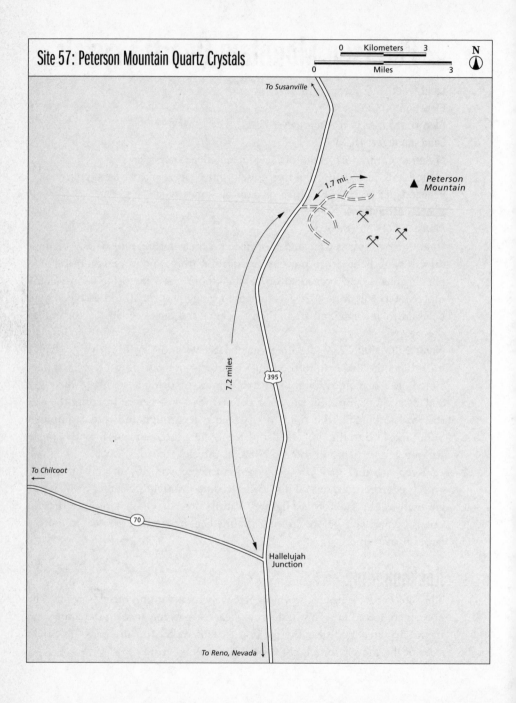

Site 57: Peterson Mountain Quartz Crystals

0   Kilometers   3

0   Miles   3

N

To Susanville

1.7 mi.

▲ Peterson Mountain

7.2 miles

395

To Chilcoot

70

Hallelujah Junction

To Reno, Nevada

Peterson Mountain quartz crystals. PHOTO BY SHEP KOSS

There are several digs on the other side of the tall mountain, the tailings piles of which yield scepter and clear quartz crystals. The easiest way to get around the mountain is to walk around the south side. Much of this mountain is under various claims on both the California and Nevada sides. Be sure to respect any claim markers.

As you walk around the mountain, you will encounter holes near several trees, the tops of which can be seen from the parking area. This is the area where pale-lavender amethyst crystals have been dug. If you don't feel up to walking around the mountain, the area around the parking loop will produce many fine specimens. Some are just lying about loose on the ground.

Use your hand cultivator and rake to locate crystals in the dry creekbed or the tailings areas on the other side of the mountain.

Antelope Lake Rose Quartz

Land type: Alpine mountains
Elevation: 7,000 feet
Best season: June to September
Land manager: USDAFS
Material: Rose quartz
Tools: Rock pick, collecting bag, chisels, crack hammer
Vehicle type: Any high-clearance vehicle
Maps: USGS Antelope Lake and Babcock Peak; USDA Plumas National Forest map
Lore: Rose quartz was prized as the stone of love and the healer of emotional pain and trauma. It was thought to bring love to the wearer and heal a broken heart.

Rose quartz takes an excellent polish. PHOTO BY GARRET ROMAINE

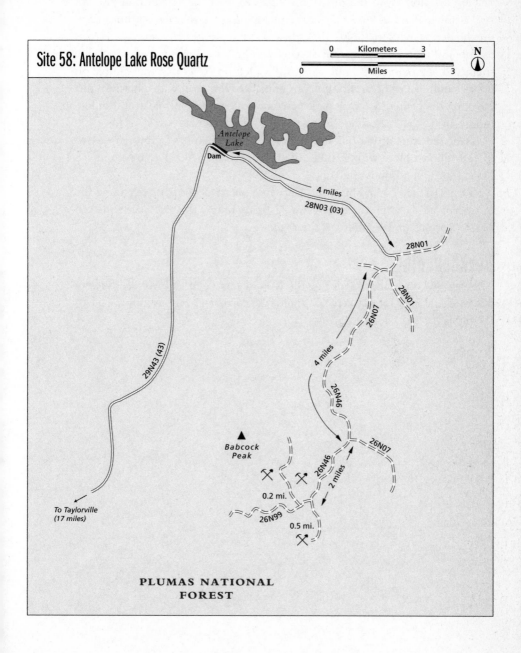

Site 58: Antelope Lake Rose Quartz

0   Kilometers   3

0   Miles   3

N

Antelope Lake

Dam

4 miles

28N03 (03)

28N01

28N01

26N07

4 miles

26N46

26N07

26N46

2 miles

0.2 mi.

Babcock Peak

29N43 (43)

To Taylorville
(17 miles)

26N99

0.5 mi.

PLUMAS NATIONAL
FOREST

Special attractions: Antelope Lake fishing, camping, and boating

Finding the site: From the junction of 29N43 (road sign states only the last two numbers) and 28N03 (03) near Antelope Lake Dam, head southeast approximately 4 miles to 26N07 (07). Head south on 26N07 for another 4 miles to 26N46 (forest service road marker now indicates entire number). Continue southwest approximately 2 miles and make a left on 26N99. Drive 0.5 mile on 26N99 and turn right (north) onto an unmarked dirt road with a berm of dirt blocking the center. You may park here and follow the pink float up the low mountain on the right side of the road to several deposits.

Near the crest of the hill and east is a sizable deposit of ruby-red quartz. Here I found a piece with a chunk of chrysoprase embedded in it. Although I looked for more, I didn't find any.

To get to the best and highest quality rose quartz deposits, drive around the dirt berm and head up the road 0.2 mile. Again follow the rose quartz float to sizable deposits on both sides of the road.

Rockhounding

This site was once under claim by the Mount Jura Gem and Mineral Society. Although their claim markers still stand, the former claims are now open to the public.

Taylorville Fossils

Land type: Hills
Elevation: 5,500 feet
Best season: May to September
Land manager: USDAFS
Material: Fossil shells
Tools: Rock pick, collecting bag
Vehicle type: Any
Special attractions: Taylorville Museum
Maps: USGS Taylorville
Lore: Fossils were worn or carried for longevity. During the Dark Ages it was believed that fossils were the remains of creatures that hadn't been taken aboard Noah's Ark and subsequently died in the Great Flood.
Finding the site: From the junction of CA 89 and CR A22 head west for 5.2 miles to and on through the small town of Taylorville. Turn left just past the rodeo grounds; continue 0.2 mile and park either on the same side of the road as the rodeo grounds or at the base of Mount Jura. Just be sure your car is well off the road. Look for a tall post with the numbers 10 43/22 in yellow paint at waist to shoulder level. The number 15 in brass will be seen farther up. This post marks where you take a steep but short hike to an area covered with green and red shale. The fossil shells (pectins) occur in the shale as molds and casts. The shells have a well-defined scallop shape of *Glyphaea punctata*.

Rockhounding

This site is easy to reach, as Mount Jura, actually a high hill, is right beside the rodeo grounds. There are a few other fossil locations near and on Mount Jura and a couple more along the southeast bank of Indian Creek. These other locations are shown on the accompanying map.

The museum in Taylorville has exhibits of local history and mining. During the weekend closest to July 4th the Mount Jura Gem and Mineral Society holds their annual show. A rodeo is also scheduled for that weekend.

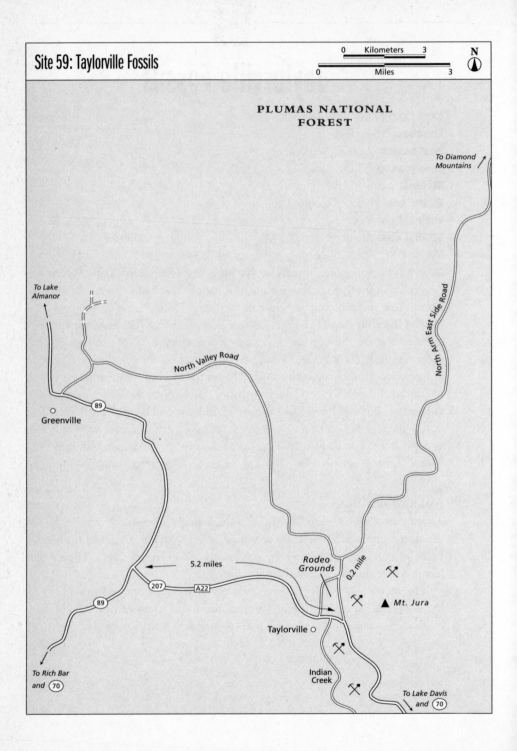

Site 59: Taylorville Fossils

0 — Kilometers — 3

0 — Miles — 3

N

PLUMAS NATIONAL FOREST

To Diamond Mountains

To Lake Almanor

North Valley Road

North Arm East Side Road

89

Greenville

5.2 miles

207 A22

Rodeo Grounds

0.2 mile

▲ Mt. Jura

89

Taylorville ○

To Rich Bar and 70

Indian Creek

To Lake Davis and 70

Buck's Lake Serpentine

Land type: Alpine mountains
Elevation: 5,700 feet
Best season: June to September
Land manager: USDAFS
Material: High-quality serpentine
Tools: Rock pick, collecting bag, chisel
Vehicle type: Any
Special attractions: Buck's Lake camping, boating, and fishing
Maps: USGS Meadow Valley; USDA Plumas National Forest map
Lore: Serpentine was worn or carried as protection against stinging and biting insects and serpents.
Finding the site: From the intersection of Buck's Lake and Silver Creek Roads, near the town of Meadow Valley, drive southwest for 1.5 miles. On the side of the road for several hundred feet is an outcropping of serpentine. Park safely off to the side at one of the wide spots. Watch carefully for cars coming around the curves, although there is a wide shoulder at the collecting area.

Rockhounding

At this site you will find high-quality palm- to watermelon-size chunks of serpentine, with little foliation.

Although much material is lying on the ground, you may wish to chisel directly from the deposit. Be careful not to let any roll out onto the road. The colors of the serpentine from this site are white, pale green, jade green, and black in varying combinations. This material is suitable for jewelry and other projects.

Site 60: Bucks Lake Serpentine

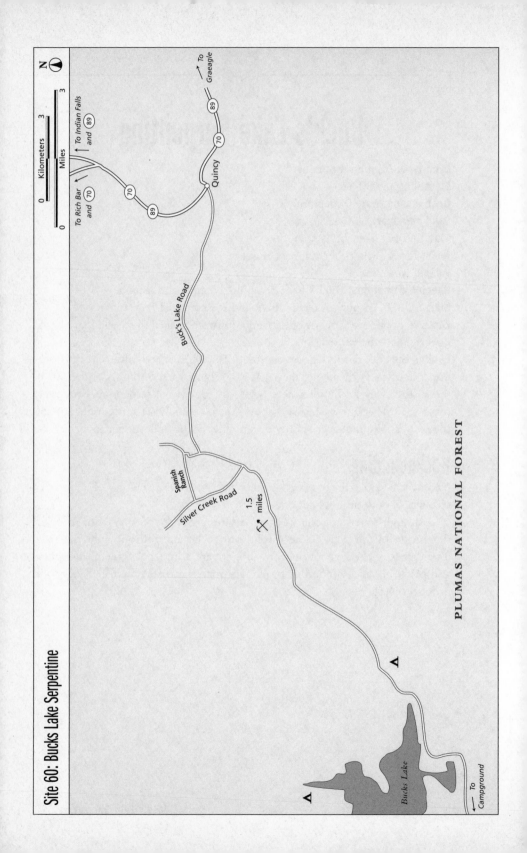

N

0   Kilometers   3

0   Miles   3

To Rich Bar and 70

To Indian Falls and 89

To Graeagle

89

70

70

89

Quincy

Buck's Lake Road

Spanish Ranch

Silver Creek Road

1.5 miles

PLUMAS NATIONAL FOREST

Bucks Lake

To Campground

Pulga Californite in Serpentine

Land type: Mountains
Elevation: 4,500 feet
GPS: N39 47.88' / W121 27.10'
Best season: May to October
Land manager: USDAFS
Material: Californite
Tools: Rock pick, collecting bag, chisel
Vehicle type: Any
Special attractions: Lake Oroville recreation
Maps: USGS Pulga
Lore: Also known as idocrase, californite was believed to stimulate loyalty and patriotism in its wearer as well as lessen skin eruptions.
Finding the site: From the intersection of CA 70 and Pulga Road, drive 0.9 mile to Camp Creek Road. The road to the site is unpaved and rocky, but low gear on your vehicle will take you up easily. Follow Camp Creek Road 0.7 mile to an outcropping of californite in serpentine on the left as you are ascending the road. The road to the site has a steep drop-off to your right, so drive carefully. About 100 yards farther up the road is a turnout where you can both turn your vehicle around and park. Low gear is recommended on the way back down to keep brakes from overheating.

Rockhounding

The material at this site has been called both idocrase and vesuvianite but is actually californite, a compact massive form of idocrase. It has also been nick-named "California jade." The californite at this location occurs as streaks and lenses in a low-quality serpentine. It is plentiful and is distinguished from the dull and foliated serpentine by its vitreous to pearly luster. The colors of this material are white, light green, dark green, jade green, beige, brown, and black. It is somewhat brittle but can be used in jewelry and tumble polished.

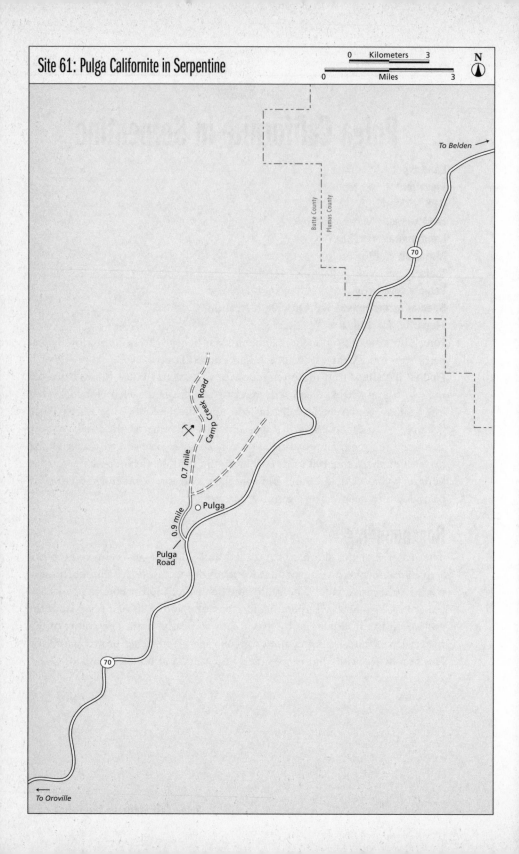

Site 61: Pulga Californite in Serpentine

0 — Kilometers — 3

0 — Miles — 3

N

To Belden →

70

Butte County
Plumas County

Camp Creek Road

0.7 mile

0.9 mile

○ Pulga

Pulga
Road

70

← To Oroville

Feather River Gold

Land type: Alpine mountains
Elevation: 3,300 feet
Best season: May to October
Land manager: Patented private claim
Material: Gold
Tools: Gold pan, shovel, trowel, rock pick, whiskbroom, long-handled screwdriver, tweezers, vial, old spoon
Vehicle type: Any
Special attractions: Nearby fishing, camping, hiking
For more information: Victor Rangel, Pine Air Resort, PO Box 15, Twain 95984; (916) 283-1730
Lore: Gold and its ownership meant wealth in historic times, much as it does today. Medicinally, gold was used to treat many physical disorders. Today in the United States it is used for the treatment of arthritis.
Finding the site: From the junction of CA 70 and CA 89 drive west about 4 miles to Twain, on your left. Just west of Twain is the Pine Air Resort. Manager Victor Rangel can lead you to panning and sluicing sites along the river. The resort also makes an excellent base camp.

Rockhounding

The Feather River has been a prolific gold producer since 1850 and is known for the size and purity of the gold nuggets found here. Many happy gold panners have shown me lovely golden nuggets ranging in size from a fraction of a pennyweight to several ounces. Reservations are recommended.

If after a visit to the Feather River you've contracted an incurable case of gold fever and yearn for information on other gold-bearing areas throughout California, you're in luck. Big Ten Inc., PO Box 321231, Cocoa Beach, FL 32932-1231, publishes maps that show everywhere gold has been found throughout the golden state—and that's a lot of places. Big Ten also publishes maps of gold locations for other states. Your own home state may be one of them! For more information, send them a stamped, self-addressed envelope; call (407) 783-4595; or visit http://goldmaps.com.

Site 62: Feather River Gold
Site 63: Feather River Serpentine

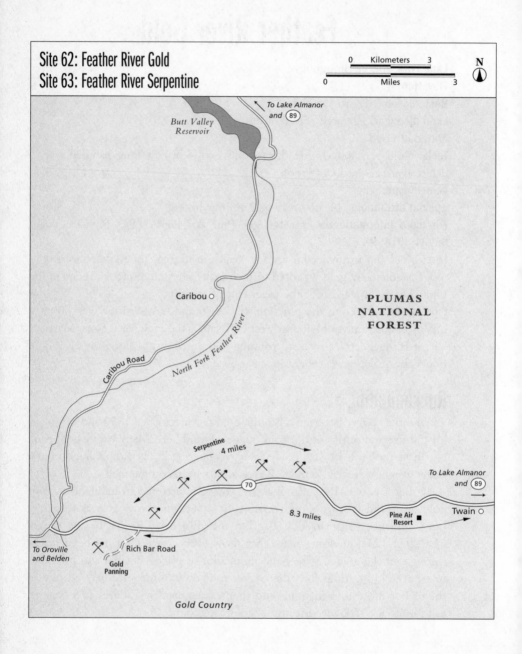

Butt Valley
Reservoir

To Lake Almanor
and (89)

Caribou ○

Caribou Road

North Fork Feather River

PLUMAS
NATIONAL
FOREST

Serpentine
4 miles

(70)

To Lake Almanor
and (89)

8.3 miles

Pine Air
Resort ■

Twain ○

To Oroville
and Belden

Rich Bar Road

Gold
Panning

Gold Country

Feather River Serpentine

(See map on page 176.)

Land type: Alpine mountains
Elevation: 3,300 feet
Best season: May to October
Land manager: USDAFS
Material: Good-grade serpentine
Tools: Rock pick, collecting bag, chisel
Vehicle type: Any
Special attractions: Feather River gold panning
Maps: USGS Caribou

Feather River serpentine. PHOTO BY SHEP KOSS

Lore: Serpentine protects its wearer against stinging insects and the bite of venomous serpents.

Finding the site: From the junction of CA 89 and CA 70, head west on CA 70 about 4 miles to Twain. Drive another 4.3 miles. From here to Rich Bar Road, spanning the next 4 miles, deposits of serpentine line the road to your right. Be careful to park off the road and not allow any serpentine to roll down onto it. Also be watchful of cars and logging trucks coming around corners.

Rockhounding

This site is best visited in conjunction with the Feather River gold site. You can both pan some gold nuggets and collect a good-quality serpentine for lapidary projects.

Serpentine tends to amass parallel to gold deposits—valuable information to keep in mind when searching for that elusive yellow metal!

Willard Creek Agate and Jasper

Land type: Alpine mountains
Elevation: 5,600 feet
GPS: N40 22.26' / W120 48.18'
Best season: June to September
Land manager: BLM
Material: Black agate, red jasper, petrified wood
Tools: Rock bag, pick
Vehicle type: Any
Special attractions: None
Maps: USGS Fredonyer Pass

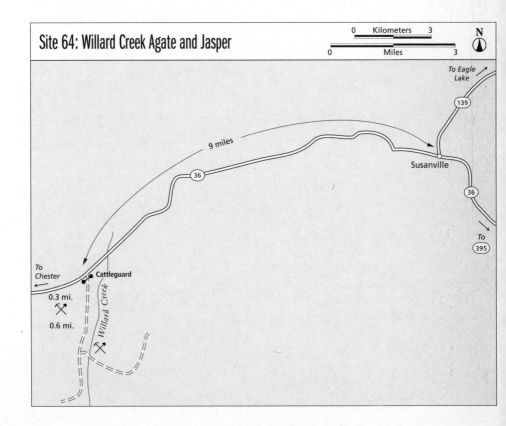

Site 64: Willard Creek Agate and Jasper

Lore: Agate and jasper were believed to protect the wearer. Red jasper was favored by archers and also thought to lower fevers. Petrified wood ensured long life.

Finding the site: From Susanville drive 9 miles west on CA 36 to Willard Creek Road. Turn left (south). Willard Creek runs north–south on the east side of the road. The best area to collect is near the creek close to the cattleguard at about 0.3 mile. If you continue down the road another 0.6 mile, the road curves and crosses Willard Creek. Here is another spot to stop and collect.

Rockhounding

This site is best visited early in the season because snowmelt and rain will bring down new material, which is not overly plentiful here. Willard Creek is a good site to visit in conjunction with the Susanville agate site.

The area where Willard Creek crosses the road is a dandy picnic spot. This site is rumored to have Apache tears, although I didn't find any on my visit.

Susanville Agates and Petrified Wood

Land type: Hills
Elevation: 4,600 feet
GPS: N40 29.30' / W120 33.25'
Best season: May to October
Land manager: BLM
Material: Agate, petrified wood, chalcedony
Tools: Rock pick, collecting bag
Vehicle type: Any
Special attractions: None
Maps: USGS Unison Mountain and Johnstonville

Lore: Petrified wood, like agate, was believed to protect the wearer and lend courage and strength. Petrified wood had the added benefit of ensuring its owner a long life. Chalcedony protected its owner against accidents and nightmares.

Finding the site: From Susanville take CA 139 north 10.3 miles to a sign on your right indicating Jack's Valley Monument. Turn left (west) onto a dirt road. To enter the collecting area, you will have to open a gate, drive through, and close the gate after you. This is cattle country, and leaving a gate open is cause for sorrow among the local ranchers. Continue on this dirt road for 1 mile. To the north, about 50 feet from the road, is a dry creekbed. Search along the creekbed and on both sides of the road for agate and petrified wood. Continue 0.4 mile farther, where there is a smaller creekbed to the south. Both quantity and quality of agate and petrified wood increase throughout the general area. Here also is found some clear to milky chalcedony.

Rockhounding

This site consists of low sage-covered hills with some large juniper trees. The collecting area is flat on both sides of the road. Although this is cattle country, none were spotted on the day my uncle and I visited this site, although much evidence attested to their presence. The petrified wood found in the dry creekbed is generally light tan with white or cream streaks and makes nice specimen pieces. At the 1.4-mile mark along the road, we found several palm-size pieces of petrified wood in colors of red, cream, brown, gray, and black. These would inspire the lapidary to works of creative jewelry making!

Site 65: Susanville Agates and Petrified Wood

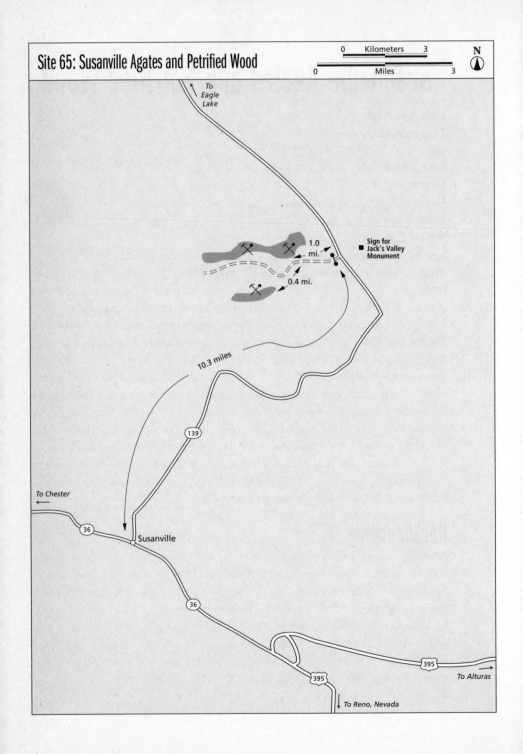

Kilometers 0 — 3

Miles 0 — 3

N

To Eagle Lake

1.0 mi.

Sign for Jack's Valley Monument

0.4 mi.

10.3 miles

139

To Chester

36

Susanville

36

395

395

To Alturas

To Reno, Nevada

Some of the chalcedony was opalized with white or cream-colored common opal and was found north of the road at the 1.4-mile mark. The agate occurs in mostly red and black.

During summer you may want to confine your collecting to the morning. In August, when I visited, daytime temperatures were about 90 degrees.

The collecting material is not abundant, but thirty minutes of easy walking will garner a bagful of good material. During the month of October, you can also gather handfuls of juniper berries. The dried berries are prized for use in seasoning meats, sauces, and gin!

Cedarville Petrified Wood

Land type: Alpine mountains
Elevation: 6,600 feet
GPS: N41 32.42' / W120 14.93'
Best season: June to August
Land manager: USDAFS
Material: Petrified wood, opalite, obsidian
Tools: Rock pick, collecting bag
Vehicle type: Any
Special attractions: None
Maps: USGS Cedarville, Warren Peak, and Payne Peak
Lore: Petrified wood was believed to promote long life for its wearer. Opalite, if worn or carried, was thought to foster serenity in accepting one's fate. Black obsidian was used in divination by gazing into its polished surface.
Finding the site: To get to Site A drive 1.5 miles south on Main Street, heading out of Cedarville toward Gerlach. Take the road to your right just south of the cemetery and drive in a westerly direction for 3.6 miles. On both sides of the road are fair amounts of petrified wood.

To get to Site B from Cedarville, take Main Street south 3.7 miles to CR 27 (or drive 2.2 miles south from Site A). Turn right onto CR 27. At 1.9 miles, on a small rise on the right, will be some opalite, small pieces of gypsum, and chalcedony. At 3 miles slow your car and scan the road edges along the slopes for occasional pieces of petrified wood, especially the areas where runoff or rocks appear to come down off the mountain. At 4.5 miles park your vehicle and walk up the slope to your right. Here the wood is at its most plentiful. The mileages to this site are progressive, so don't reset your mileage indicator.

To reach Site C, head west out of Cedarville from the intersection of Main Street and CA 299. Drive 4.9 miles and take the road to your left where a sign indicates skiing. At 0.1 mile follow the road to the left. (Continuing straight would put you at a locked gate.) The road curves to your left. After an additional 0.1 mile, stop. The right-hand side of the road is littered with coal-black obsidian, some of which has a white or gray banding, and occasional pieces of petrified wood.

Site 66: Cedarville Petrified Wood

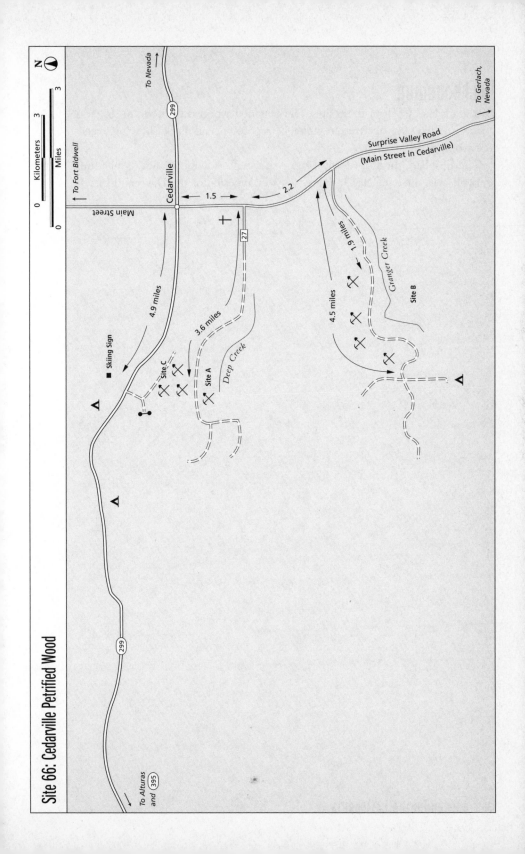

Rockhounding

Dirt roads lead to all of these sites. The petrified wood is of medium to good quality and has been agatized in white, beige, brown, and black, showing excellent wood grain.

The obsidian, though mostly black with gray or white bands, is plentiful and will make nice jewelry. It will whet your appetite for the Davis and Lassen Creeks sites.

Davis Creek Obsidian Varieties

Land type: Alpine mountains
Elevation: 7,000 feet
GPS: N41 43.54' / W120 16.89'
Best season: June to August
Land manager: USDAFS
Material: Rainbow, mahogany, red-and-black, silver-and-gray obsidian
Tools: Rock pick, collecting bags, gloves, eye protection
Vehicle type: Any
Special attractions: None
Maps: USGS Davis Creek
Lore: Rainbow obsidian is thought to bring light, love, and joy to its owner. Mahogany obsidian was worn to help in attaining physical strength and achieving goals. Red-and-black obsidian assists one's libido and harmonizes the relations between men and women. Gray or silver-and-gray obsidian was used in shamanic healing rituals and to assist in astral travel.

Finding the site: In order to collect at any of these sites, you must first obtain a permit at Davis Creek Mercantile, in the tiny burg of Davis Creek. The permit is free but necessary to avoid penalties imposed by the forest service. The folks at the Davis Creek Mercantile can provide you with the permit and are helpful with information on the sites. They also have additional maps upon request.

To get to Site A drive north of Davis Creek Mercantile 1 block on US 395. Turn right and drive 0.8 mile to a triple fork. The left fork goes toward a gate and private land; the right fork heads to the cemetery. Stay to the center. From this point on, you will find lots of black obsidian to the right, should you desire to stop and collect.

Site B has the famous rainbow obsidian, as well as a gray-and-silver variety. Both contain the desired rainbow effects. To reach this site drive 1.5 miles from the triple fork. Ignore the road to the right and drive another 1.2 miles. Take this right and drive another 1.5 miles. Just before the road curves around to the right, you will see a steep track heading up the side of a hill. Just past this track there is a spot to your left to pull off and park your car. The small creek here will be a source of refreshment when you return from your hike up the hill. The track up to the site is too steep to drive, and once at the top, there is no place to turn around. Also, the track is littered with sharp shards of obsidian.

Davis Creek obsidian chunk and needles. PHOTO BY SHEP KOSS

To get to Site C and the mahogany and red-and-black obsidian, return 1.5 miles to where you turned off to collect rainbow obsidian and head 1.2 miles farther up this main road. Ignore the road to the left and continue another 2.2 miles, ignoring the road to the right. Another 0.6 mile will bring you to the mahogany and red-and-black obsidian site. The collecting material lines both sides of the road and up the slope to your right, as well as down the slope to your left.

Rockhounding

Reaching Site B will require commitment. The climb is steep, and just when you think you're going to crest the hill (a very tall hill), you find you're not quite there yet. The climb is only about 0.3-plus mile, but it is steep. The climb is further complicated near the top by many sharp pieces of obsidian and pine needles that lie deep under the pine trees. Both make for treacherous walking. The pine needles are slippery, and should you fall you will be certain to cut

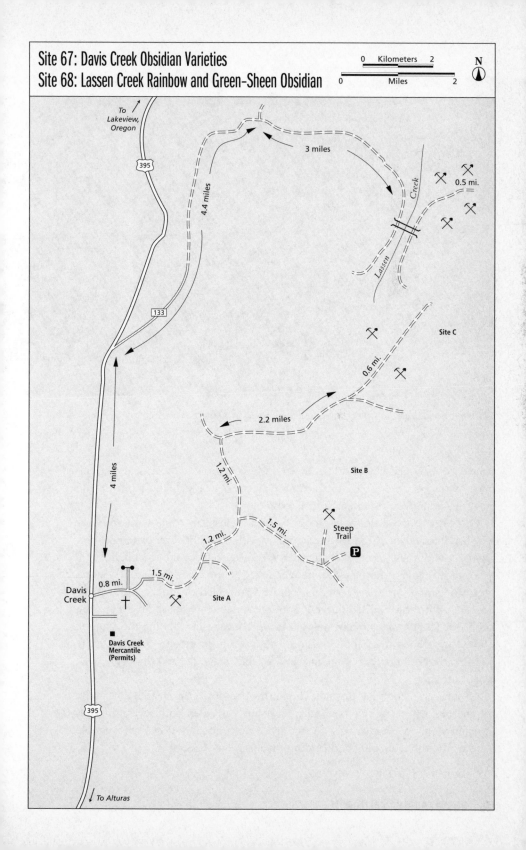

Site 67: Davis Creek Obsidian Varieties
Site 68: Lassen Creek Rainbow and Green-Sheen Obsidian

0 Kilometers 2

0 Miles 2

N

To Lakeview, Oregon

395

3 miles

4.4 miles

0.5 mi.

Lassett Creek

133

Site C

0.6 mi.

2.2 miles

Site B

1.2 mi.

1.5 mi.

Steep Trail

4 miles

1.2 mi.

P

0.8 mi.

1.5 mi.

Davis Creek

Site A

Davis Creek Mercantile (Permits)

395

To Alturas

Obsidian needles are an interesting collectible. PHOTO BY GARRET ROMAINE

yourself on the glasslike obsidian. It would be advisable to wear heavy hiking boots with contoured soles for maximum traction, heavy denim pants in case you fall, and gloves to protect your hands.

Once up, you will find what looks like black obsidian, some with white or gray banding and another variety that is gray with cream or silver banding. Look again; some of these pieces will glimmer with iridescent rainbows of light.

You will have to develop "rainbow vision." It took me about thirty minutes of seemingly fruitless searching before I stumbled on this technique. Try to search with the sun behind you. Sunlight enhances your ability to see the rainbows. Then look carefully, walking stooped over and scanning the ground. Once I developed my rainbow vision, I found one piece after another, fairly consistently. Not all pieces contain rainbows, but many do, and the trip is well worth the hike.

Obsidian is plentiful at this site. The return trip down the steep track can be treacherous. My technique for returning to my car, laden with several pounds of prime rainbow obsidian, was to zigzag as I descended. In this way I was able to return without slipping and landing on sharp obsidian.

At Site C you will find lovely pieces of mahogany obsidian, some with black flecks, and red-and-black obsidian, which is basically a reverse coloration of the mahogany variety. Both are beautiful and make lovely cabochons, belt buckles, and other lapidary creations, as well as great specimens.

Also at this location you will find the unusual obsidian "needles"—elongated shards of obsidian in various lengths. Davis Creek Mercantile has some almost 1 foot long on display. Most of the needles are only several inches long, but they are unique and therefore worth collecting while at this site.

Be sure to wear gloves when collecting obsidian. Also wear eye protection if you decide to use your rock pick to chip or break the material.

One more caution: Plan your trips to this area not much later than August. This is high elevation, and winter comes early and stays late in this part of the country. This is the area where a young couple and their baby were lost when their truck broke down in deep snow and they attempted to walk out. They eventually were rescued when the father walked out for help. The area is mostly farm and cattle country and is very sparsely populated. Let someone know when you are going in, how long you'll be, and when you expect to return.

Lassen Creek Rainbow and Green-Sheen Obsidian

(See the map on page 189.)

Land type: Alpine mountains
Elevation: 6,000 feet
GPS: N41 50.10' / W120 17.81'
Best season: June to August
Land manager: USDAFS
Material: Rainbow obsidian, green-sheen obsidian
Tools: Rock pick, collecting bag, gloves, eye protection
Vehicle type: Any

The more you get out, the better you get at packing just the essentials.
PHOTO BY GARRET ROMAINE

Special attractions: None

Maps: USGS Sugar Hill

Lore: Black obsidian was used by most ancient cultures for divination. Rainbow obsidian additionally contained the vibration of joy, while green-sheen obsidian was worn to attract wealth and health.

Finding the site: From Davis Creek head north on US 395 for 4 miles. Turn right onto CR 133 and drive north for 4.4 miles. Turn right and drive 3 miles to the bridge. Cross the bridge and turn left. Drive 0.5 mile to the obsidian site.

Be sure to get all your state and federal passes at the beginning of the rockhounding season. PHOTO BY SHEP KOSS

Rockhounding

At 0.5 mile you will see numerous shallow pits on both sides of the road. Obsidian will be scattered all over; the material is abundant here. From a distance all the obsidian at this site appears to be plain black. Closer inspection reveals both rainbow and green-sheen obsidian. Keeping the sun to your back will help you locate both types. The rainbow obsidian is more plentiful than the sheen, but you need only look a short time to find several pieces of the sheen.

In some cases it is helpful to use your rock pick to chip the edges of the obsidian in order to reveal a fresh surface. Be sure to wear eye protection when doing this; obsidian fragments can be nearly invisible and very sharp. This is where I got a sliver of obsidian in my finger because I was not wearing my gloves as I should have been.

There is also supposed to be gold-sheen, blue-sheen, and silver-sheen obsidian at this site, but I did not find any of those on my trip.

Shasta Area Copper Minerals

Land type: Hills
Elevation: 4,100 feet
GPS: N41 32.90' / W122 15.45'
Best season: May to September
Land manager: USDAFS
Material: Chalcocite, chalcopyrite, malachite, chrysocolla
Tools: Rock pick, collecting bag
Vehicle type: Any
Special attractions: Mount Shasta scenic vistas and camping; Shasta Lake limestone caverns
Maps: USGS Juniper Flat and The Whaleback
Lore: No lore is available on chalcocite or chalcopyrite. Malachite, worn or carried, was believed to assist one during times of change or disruption. It was also thought to facilitate an understanding of the mind/body link in illness. Chrysocolla was worn for its calming and energizing properties.
Finding the site: The road to this site is located 0.3-plus mile southwest of the junction of CA 97 and CR A12. Turn north onto Yellow Butte Road and continue 1 mile. Turn onto the road to your left and drive 0.1 mile.

Rockhounding

Dark gray chalcocite, metallic chalcopyrite, green malachite, and bluish green chrysocolla are found on the dumps of an old copper mine. All four copper minerals make excellent specimens for a mineral collection. Rarely, lapidary-grade malachite and chrysocolla can be collected as well, although the pieces are small. For best results, use your rock pick to dig into the tailings.

Mount Shasta, south on I-5 from the collecting site, is a beautiful area. Around the small town of Mount Shasta are several campgrounds. Bookstores in town carry a wide variety of books on Mount Shasta's mystical history.

The mountain has been the site of many strange sightings of ancient Lemurians and UFOs. Native Americans have many legends concerning the mystical nature of this area.

Farther south down I-5 is Shasta Lake. Camping and boating may be enjoyed here. The feature of most interest is the limestone caverns where visitors can see large limestone galleries filled with stalactites and stalagmites of interesting proportions. Guided tours are available.

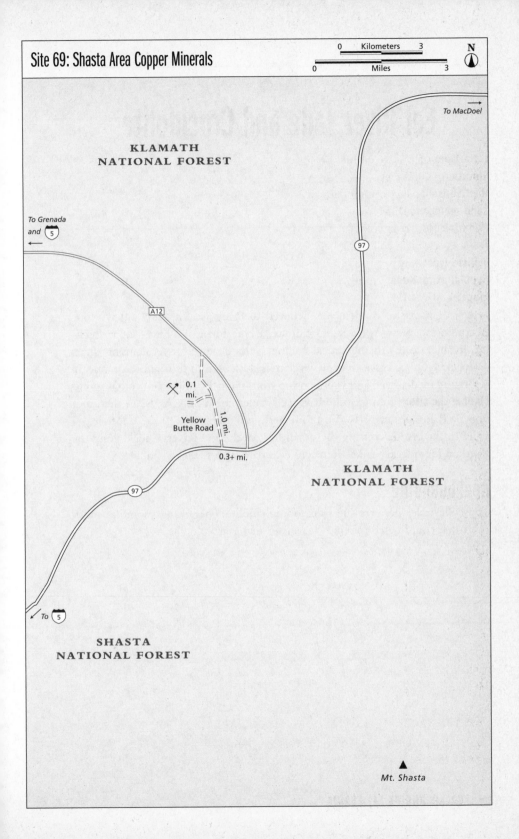

0   Kilometers   3

0   Miles   3

N

KLAMATH
NATIONAL FOREST

To MacDoel

To Grenada
and 5

97

A12

⚒ 0.1
mi.

1.0 mi.

Yellow
Butte Road

0.3+ mi.

97

KLAMATH
NATIONAL FOREST

To 5

SHASTA
NATIONAL FOREST

Mt. Shasta

Eel River Jade and Crocidolite

Land type: Oak-covered hills
Elevation: 3,000 feet
Best season: May to October
Land manager: BLM
Material: Jade, crocidolite
Tools: Rock pick, collecting bag
Vehicle type: Any
Special attractions: None
Maps: USGS Mina

Lore: Jade, worn or carried, was believed to bring wealth, luck and wisdom. According to New Age lore, crocidolite, a blue form of asbestos or riebeckite, enhances one's mathematical abilities. (Good news for recalcitrant check balancers.) On a less-mundane level it heightens intuition and aids one in separating media hype and salesmanship from the truly important things in life.

Finding the site: From Covelo drive 12.4 miles north on CA 162 to the junction of Bald Mountain Road. From here continue on CA 162 another 4.7 miles to the bridge crossing the north fork of the Eel River. Check along the riverbed for jade in shades from white to dark green and crocidolite.

Rockhounding

The collectibles here are the jade and crocidolite. There is also some purplish chert that could be considered "leaverite" material.

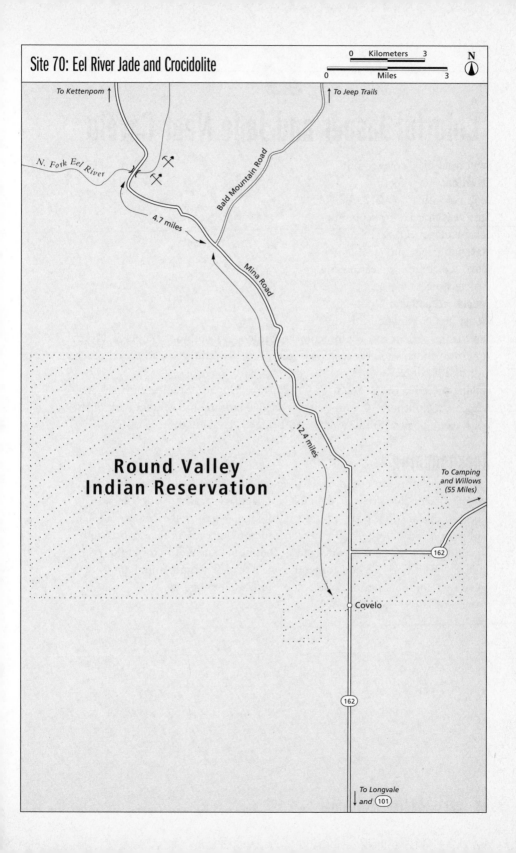

Kilometers

0   3

0   Miles   3

N

To Kettenpom

To Jeep Trails

N. Fork Eel River

Bald Mountain Road

4.7 miles

Mina Road

12.4 miles

Round Valley
Indian Reservation

To Camping
and Willows
(55 Miles)

162

Covelo

162

To Longvale
and 101

Colorful Jasper and Jade Near Covelo

Land type: Oak–covered hills
Elevation: 3,000 feet
GPS: N39 49.49' / W123 05.49'
Best season: May to September
Land manager: USDAFS
Material: Jasper and jade
Tools: Rock pick, collecting bag
Vehicle type: Any
Special attractions: None
Maps: USGS Newhouse Ridge
Lore: Jasper was worn for protection in battle and to promote courage. North American Indians used it in rain-bringing rituals. Jade attracted wealth, luck, love, and wisdom.
Finding the site: In the town of Covelo take CA 162 heading north. It will swing east. Continue 10.5 miles to the bridge crossing the Middle Fork of the Eel River. The area to the west of the bridge is the best area to collect.

Rockhounding

The jasper at this site comes in red, yellow, brown, and rusty red. White patterning makes this material desirable for lapidary projects. Jade can also be found in this area but takes a bit more looking. Much of the jade found here is of poor quality. However, if you plan your trip for early in the season, winter rain and snowmelt coming down from the mountains will restore both jasper and jade quantities. The jade comes in several shades, ranging from light to dark green or a combination of these colors, with some white pieces.

Site 71: Colorful Jasper and Jade Near Covelo

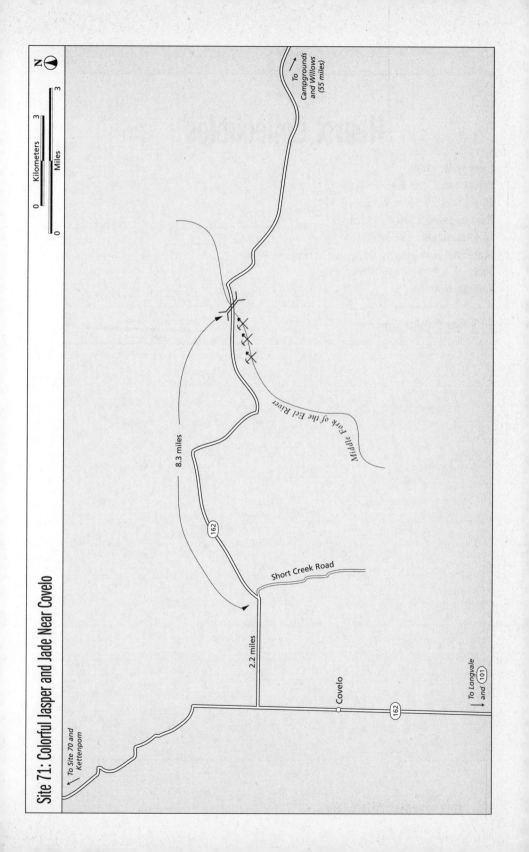

N

Kilometers
0   3

Miles
0   3

To Site 70 and
Kettenpom

162

2.2 miles

8.3 miles

Short Creek Road

Covelo

162

To Longvale
and 101

Middle Fork of the Eel River

To
Campgrounds
and Willows
(55 miles)

SITE 72

Hearst Collectibles

Land type: Hills
Elevation: 2,200 feet
GPS: N39 29.65' / W123 12.57'
Best season: April to October
Land manager: USDAFS
Material: Banded rhyolite, jade, actinolite, jasper
Tools: Rock pick, collecting bag
Vehicle type: Any

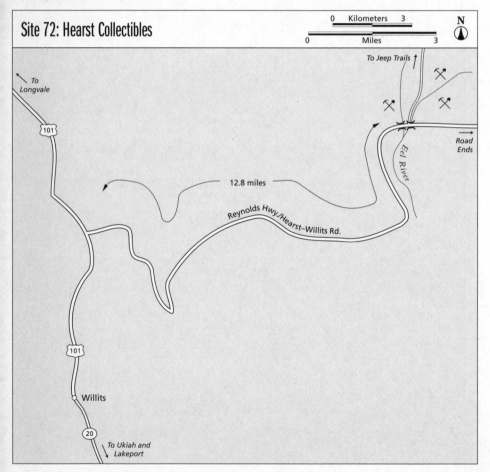

Site 72: Hearst Collectibles

Special attractions: Mendocino County Museum in Willits

Maps: USGS Willits and Foster Mountain

Lore: The ancients used rhyolite in balms for curing circulatory and skin problems. Jade promotes wealth, luck, love, and wisdom. Actinolite has similar, although milder, properties to jade but also aids in promoting brotherhood.

Finding the site: From Willits head north on US 101 a short distance to Reynolds Highway. Turn right. Drive 12.8 miles on this road, which becomes Hearst-Willits Road. Stay to the left. (If you turn right you will wind up back in Willits near the airport.) Hearst-Willits Road will take you to the bridge that crosses the Eel River. Park and search up and down the river area.

Rockhounding

This site is another that is best visited early in the season, after spring runoff renews the availability of collecting material. This is the time when larger pieces of jade will more likely be found.

Banded rhyolite, actinolite in green hues, jade in white and green, and colorful jasper in warm red, orange, yellow, and white are the collectibles of interest here.

The Mendocino County Museum offers visitors a look at the history of Mendocino County from early Native American cultures to the present day. There is also a botanical garden containing indigenous plant species.

Black Butte Reservoir Showy Jasper

Land type: Hills
Elevation: 3,400 feet
GPS: N39 48.77' / W122 21.73'
Best season: April to November
Land manager: BLM
Material: Jasper, agate, petrified wood
Tools: Rock pick, collecting bag

Remember, you can collect up to 250 pounds a year of petrified wood.
PHOTO BY GARRET ROMAINE

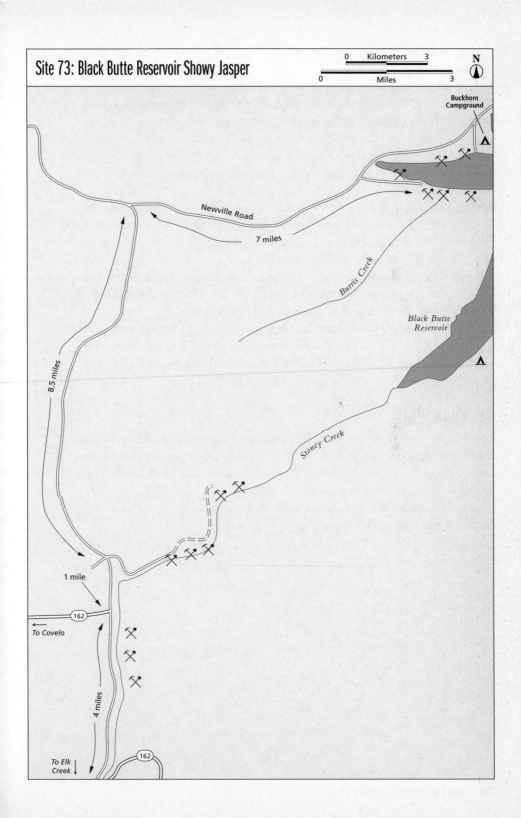

Site 73: Black Butte Reservoir Showy Jasper

Kilometers
0   3

Miles
0   3

N

Buckhorn
Campground

Newville Road

7 miles

Burris Creek

Black Butte
Reservoir

8.5 miles

Stoney Creek

1 mile

162

To Covelo

4 miles

To Elk
Creek

162

Vehicle type: Any

Special attractions: Black Butte Reservoir boating and camping

Maps: USGS Chrome, Julian Rocks, Sehorn Creek, and Black Butte Dam

Lore: Jasper and agate were worn for protection and courage. Red jasper was prized by archers, while green was inscribed with a magic symbol and worn for digestive problems. Jasper was an important ingredient in Native American rain-bringing rituals. Petrified wood was believed to bestow long life on its wearer.

Finding the site: From the town of Elk Creek take the Lagoda-Stoneyford Road north for 0.5 mile. From the junction of this road, which runs along Stoney Creek and CA 162, you can collect some jasper if you continue east along Stoney Creek for 3.5 miles. At the 3.5-mile mark you will encounter CA 162 coming in from the west. Continue north another 1 mile. You will see a road to the right, which heads east. Jasper can be collected along this road, which follows Stoney Creek in an east-northeast direction.

For more jasper, some agate, and petrified wood, backtrack to Lagoda-Stoneyford Road and continue north about 8.5 miles to Newville Road. Turn right and head for Black Butte Reservoir, another 7 miles. All along the shores of the reservoir you can find jasper, agate, and petrified wood.

Rockhounding

Good collecting can be had near the Buckhorn Campground and the head of Burris Creek at the east side of the reservoir. You may discover, as I did, that some of your jasper samples have inclusions of marcasite. Most of the jasper and agate come in red, orange, yellow, and green.

When the water level in the reservoir drops at summer's end and into the fall, more material can be found along the shoreline.

Goat Mountain Moss Agate

Land type: Alpine mountains
Elevation: 6,000 feet
Best season: June to September
Land manager: USDAFS
Material: Moss agate
Tools: Rock pick, collecting bag
Vehicle type: Four-wheel drive or high-clearance two-wheel drive
Special attractions: Letts Lake recreation
Maps: USGS Fouts Spring; Mendocino National Forest map
Lore: This stone was thought to ensure a green thumb to one wishing to plant a garden. It was also believed to heal the pain of a stiff neck and to assist in locating lost treasure.

Amanite muscaria, *a deadly mushroom from the pine forests. Pretty to photograph, but very poisonous.* PHOTO BY GARRET ROMAINE

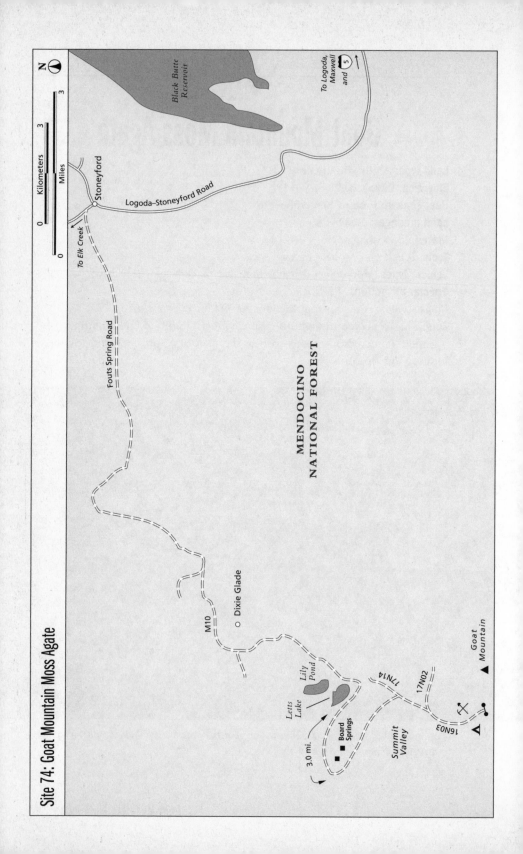

Site 74: Goat Mountain Moss Agate

Finding the site: Exit I-5 at the Maxwell off-ramp in the town of Maxwell and drive west through town. Remain on this road. You will pass through the town of Logoda to the town of Stoneyford. Turn left at the forest service workstation and continue on Fouts Spring Road (M10). Stay on M10 to Dixie Glade; turn left and head toward Letts Lake. Pass the lake and continue 3 miles to the Board Springs housing tract. At the first two-way turn go left and continue 0.2-plus mile. Take the road to the left, which will go up the hill to a log landing. Turn right. Turn left on Second Way and drive through the housing tract. Second Way becomes Crossing Road. Follow this road toward Summit Valley. Take 17N14 to 17N02 to 16N03. You should see a sign indicating Goat Mountain Lookout. On your right will be a small, unimproved campground just before you reach a gate. The moss agate is located across from the camp on the sides of a bare mountain.

Rockhounding

This site comes courtesy of Herman Schob, a friend and occasional rock-hounding partner. It is located approximately 50 miles from the town of Maxwell. You'll be driving mostly dirt roads, some regularly maintained and some not, from the town of Stoneyford to the collecting site.

The moss agate is translucent to snow white, with plentiful black inclusions of mosslike dendrites and containing occasional small pockets of drusy quartz crystals. Some of the material has mustard yellow speckling. It makes fabulous cabochons and is great for tumbling.

Although not a day trip, this site would be great for a weekend or weeklong trip. A historic marker at Letts Lake marks this as the site of an old gold claim. Fishing and camping are available at Letts Lake.

Pack a picnic lunch for this site. Herman says the view from here to the Sacramento Valley and yonder buttes is spectacular!

Appendix A: Sources Used for This Guide

Chesterman, Charles W. *The Audubon Society Field Guide to North American Rocks and Minerals.* New York: Alfred A. Knopf, Inc., 1978.

Cunningham, Scott. *Crystal, Gem & Metal Magic.* St. Paul, Minnesota: Llewellyn Publications, 1991.

Melody. *Love Is in the Earth: A Kaleidoscope of Crystals.* Wheatridge, Colorado: Earth-Love Publishing House, 1991.

Prinz, Martin, George Harlow, and Joseph Peters, eds. *Simon & Schuster's Guide to Rocks and Minerals.* New York: Simon & Schuster, 1977.

Ransom, Jay Ellis. *Fossils in America.* New York: Harper & Row Publishers, 1964.

Sharp, Robert P., and Allen F. Glazner. *Geology Underfoot in Southern California.* Missoula, Montana: Mountain Press, 1993.

Sorrell, Charles A. *Minerals of the World.* Racine, Wisconsin: Western Publishing Co., 1973.

Tarbuck, Edward J., and Frederick K. Lutgens. *The Earth, an Introduction to Physical Geology.* Columbus, Ohio: Charles E. Merrill Publishing Co., 1984.

Appendix B:
Further Reading and Information

Baylor, Byrd. *Everybody Needs a Rock.* New York: Macmillan Publishing Co., 1974.

Chocron, Daya Sarai. *Healing with Crystals and Gemstones.* York Beach, Maine: Samuel Weiser, Inc., 1986.

Gleason, Sterling. *Ultraviolet Guide to Minerals.* Toronto, Canada: D. Van Nostrand Co. Ltd., 1960.

Jewelry Crafts magazine. Ventura, California.

Lapidary Journal. Devon, Pennsylvania.

Overbey, Charles. *Big Ten's Gold Maps of California.* Cocoa Beach, Florida.

Rock & Gem magazine. Ventura, California.

Ryan, A. H. *The Weekend Rock Hound.* Pico Rivera, California: Gem Guide Books Co., 1970.

Sinkankas, John. *Prospecting for Gemstones and Minerals.* New York: Van Nostrand Reinhold Co., 1961.

Appendix C: Rockhound Clubs and Organizations

Rock and mineral clubs provide rockhounds with a variety of services, such as the companionship of like-minded people. They offer weekend field trips, an annual show where members can display and sell their jewelry or special finds, and interesting programs and workshops. Many extend training in lapidary and silversmithing skills. Some clubs have their own claims, which are open to collection for members, or the members may have knowledge of collecting sites that are not widely known. Rockhounds can greatly widen their horizons by joining a rockhounding group.

Amador County Gem & Mineral
Society
5 Broad St.
Sutter Creek, CA 95685

American Opal Society
PO Box 382
Anaheim, CA 92815

American River Gem & Mineral
Society
PO Box 1376
Fair Oaks, CA 95661

Antelope Valley Gem & Mineral
Club
PO Box 69
Lancaster, CA 93584

Antiock Lapidary Club
PO Box 91
Antioch, CA 94509

Autonetics Gem & Mineral Club
5425 Vista Linda
Yorba Linda, CA 92687

Bear Gulch Rock Club
PO Box 304
Ontario, CA 91764

Berkeley Gem & Mineral Society
PO Box 755
Berkeley, CA 94701

Boulder Buster Geology Study
Group
245 East Thomson Ave.
Sonoma, CA 95476

Cal City–Edwards Gem & Mineral
Club
PO Box 2307
California City, CA 93504

Calaveras Gem & Mineral Society
PO Box 517
Angeles Camp, CA 95222

Campbell Gem & Mineral Club
PO Box 217
Campbell, CA 95009-0217

Capistrano Valley Rock & Mineral Club
PO Box 279
San Clemente, CA 92674

Carmel Valley Gem & Mineral Society
PO Box 5846
Carmel, CA 93921

Carmichael Gem & Mineral Society
2040 Waterford Rd.
Sacramento, CA 95815

Centinela Valley Gem & Mineral Club
5316 West 82nd St.
Los Angeles, CA 90045

Coalinga Rockhounds Society
PO Box 652
Coalinga, CA 93210

Conejo Gem & Mineral Club
PO Box 723
Newbury Park, CA 91319

Contra Costa Mineral & Gem Society
PO Box 4667
Walnut Creek, CA 94596

Culver City Rock & Mineral Club
PO Box 3324
Culver City, CA 90231

Davis-Woodland Gem & Mineral Society
630 East St.
Davis, CA 95616

Del-Air Rockhounds Club
PO Box 7618
Van Nuys, CA 91409

Delvers Gem & Mineral Society
Box 4115
Downey, CA 90241

East Bay Mineral Society
2506 High St.
Oakland, CA 94601

Eastern Sierra Rock & Mineral Society
PO Box 1156
Mammoth Lakes, CA 93546

El Cajon Valley Gem & Mineral Society
PO Box 451
El Cajon, CA 92022

El Dorado County Mineral & Gem Society
PO Box 950
Placerville, CA 95667

Estero Bay Gem & Mineral Society
PO Box 248
Morro Bay, CA 93443

Faceters Guild of Northern California
4270 Silver Crest Ave.
Sacramento, CA 95821

Faceters Guild of Southern California
PO Box 8890-436
Fountain Valley, CA 92708

Fairfield Lapidary Society
PO Box 603
Fairfield, CA 94533

Fallbrook Gem & Mineral Society
PO Box 62
Fallbrook, CA 92028

Foothill Gem & Mineral Society
6265 Altura Ave.
La Crescenta, CA 91214

Forester Rockhounds #779
4680 Mt. Armet Dr.
San Diego, CA 92117

Fossils for Fun Society
1449 Sebastian Way
Sacramento, CA 95864

Fresno Gem & Mineral Society
340 West Olive
Fresno, CA 93728

Galileo Gem Guild
199 Museum Way
South San Francisco, CA 94080

Gem Carvers Guild
230 Churchill Glen
Sierra Madre, CA 91024

Gemological Society of San Diego
PO Box 1448
Spring Valley, CA 91979

Glendale Verdugo Gem & Mineral
Society
PO Box 265
Montrose, CA 91021

Glendora Gems
859 East Sierra Ave.
Glendora, CA 91740

Golden Empire Mineral Society
PO Box 1212
Chico, CA 95927

Hollister Gem & Lapidary Club
PO Box 438
Hollister, CA 95024

Hollywood Lapidary & Mineral
Society
2529 West Temple St.
Los Angeles, CA 90026

Humboldt Gem & Mineral Society
PO Box 1075
Eureka, CA 95501

Imperial Valley Gem & Mineral
Society
PO Box 1721
El Centro, CA 92244

Indian Wells Gem & Mineral Society
PO Box 1481
China Lake, CA 93555

Islanders Gem & Mineral Society
PO Box 21007
El Cajon, CA 92021

Kaiser Rock & Gem Club
15380 Orchid St.
Fontana, CA 92325

Kern County Mineral Society
11800 Brockridge Court
Bakersfield, CA 93305

Kings Stonecrafters
1325 Beulah St.
Hanford, CA 93238

La Puente Gem & Mineral Club
PO Box 647
La Puente, CA 91744

Lake County Diamond & Mineral
Society
PO Box 272
Nice, CA 95464

Lake Elsinore Gem & Mineral
Society
33040 Dowman
Lake Elsinore, CA 92530

Lassen Gem & Mineral Society
PO Box 161
Susanville, CA 96130

Livermore Valley Lithophiles
PO Box 626
Livermore, CA 94550

Lodi Gem & Mineral Society
PO Box 572
Lodi, CA 95241

Long Beach Mineral & Gem Society
PO Box 4082
Long Beach, CA 90804

Los Angeles Lapidary Society
2517 Federal Ave.
Los Angeles, CA 90064

Los Angeles Mineralogical Society
228 South Oxford Ave.
Los Angeles, CA 90004

Marin Mineral Society
PO Box 150345
San Rafael, CA 94915-0345

Mariposa Gem & Mineral Club
PO Box 753
Mariposa, CA 95338

Mendocino Coast Gem & Mineral
Society
PO Box 868
Fort Bragg, CA 95437

Merced Gem & Mineral Society
PO Box 607
Merced, CA 95340

Mineral & Gem Society of Castro
Valley
PO Box 2145
Castro Valley, CA 94546

Mineral Research Society of
Southern California
4759 Blackthorne Ave.
Long Beach, CA 90808

Mineralogical Society of Southern
California
PO Box 41027
Pasadena, CA 91104

Modoc Gem & Mineral Society
PO Box 465
Alturas, CA 96101

Mojave Desert Gem & Mineral
Society
25647 West Main
Barstow, CA 92311

Mojave Mineralogical Society
PO Box 511
Boron, CA 93596

Monrovia Rockhounds
PO Box 553
Monrovia, CA 91016

Monterey Bay Mineral Society
PO Box 12
Salinas, CA 93901

Mother Lode Mineral Society
PO Box 1263
Modesto, CA 95353

Mother Lode Mineralites
PO Box 9498
Auburn, CA 95604

Mt. Jura Gem & Mineral Society
PO Box 194
Taylorville, CA 95983

Napa Valley Rock & Gem Society
PO Box 404
Napa, CA 94559

Needles Gem & Mineral Club
PO Box 762
Needles, CA 92363

Nevada County Gem & Mineral
Society
PO Box 565
Nevada City, CA 95959

North Island Gem & Mineral
Society
PO Box 20772
El Cajon, CA 92021

North Orange County Gem &
Mineral Society
PO Box 653
La Habra, CA 90633

Northern California Mineralogical
Association
PO Box 27
Point Arena, CA 95468

Northrop Recreation Gem &
Mineral Club
1 Northrop Ave.
Hawthorne, CA 90025

Orange Belt Mineralogical Society
PO Box 5642
San Bernardino, CA 92412

Orange Coast Mineral & Lapidary
Society
PO Box 10175
Costa Mesa, CA 92626

Orange County 49ers
PO Box 781
Midway City, CA 92655

Orcutt Mineral Society
PO Box 106
Santa Maria, CA 93454

Oxnard Gem & Mineral Society
PO Box 246
Oxnard, CA 93032

Pajaro Valley Rockhounds
361 Manor Ave.
Watsonville, CA 95076

Palmdale Gem & Mineral Society
PO Box 900279
Palmdale, CA 93590

Palomar Gem & Mineral Club
PO Box 1583
Escondido, CA 92033

Palos Verdes Gem & Mineral Society
PO Box 686
Lomita, CA 90717

Paradise Gem & Mineral Club
PO Box 692
Paradise, CA 95967

Pasadena Lapidary Society
PO Box 5025
Pasadena, CA 91117

Peninsula Gem & Geology Society
PO Box 952
Los Altos, CA 94022

Pomona Rockhounds
PO Box 194
Pomona, CA 91769

Porterville Area Gem & Mineral
Society
10 Olive Dr.
Porterville, CA 93257

Ramona Adventure & Treasure
Seekers
PO Box 597
Hemet, CA 92546-0597

Rancho Bernardo Rockhounds
16955 Bernardo Oaks Dr.
San Diego, CA 92128

Rancho Santa Margarita Gem &
Mineral Society
PO Box 355
San Luis Rey, CA 92068

Red Bluff Lapidarists
PO Box 435
Red Bluff, CA 96080

Redwood Gem & Mineral Society
PO Box 203
Santa Rosa, CA 95402

Riverside Treasure Hunters
16454 Washington Dr.
Fontana, CA 92335

Rockatomics Gem & Mineral
Society
PO Box 346
Canoga Park, CA 91307

Rockcrafters Club
2540 Orange Ave.
La Crescenta, CA 91214

Roseville Rock Rollers
PO Box 212
Roseville, CA 95678

Sacramento Mineral Society
PO Box 160544
Sacramento, CA 95816

Sacramento Valley Detecting Buffs
4910 Ortega St.
Sacramento, CA 95820

San Diego Lapidary Society
5641 Mildred St.
San Diego, CA 92110

San Diego Mineral & Gem Society
Spanish Village, Balboa Park
San Diego, CA 92101

San Dieguito Gem & Mineral
Society
PO Box 863
Encinitas, CA 92024

San Fernando Valley Mineral & Gem
Society
PO Box 21
North Hollywood, CA 91603

San Francisco Gem & Mineral
Society
4234 Judah St.
San Francisco, CA 94122

San Gorgonio Mineral & Gem
Society
PO Box 424
Banning, CA 92220

San Luis Obispo Gem & Mineral
Club
PO Box 563
San Luis, CA 93406

San Pablo Bay Gem & Mineral
Society
PO Box 636
San Pablo, CA 94806

Santa Ana Rock & Mineral Club
PO Box 51
Santa Ana, CA 92702

Santa Barbara Mineral & Gem
Society
PO Box 815
Santa Barbara, CA 93102

Santa Clara Valley Gem & Mineral
Society
PO Box 54
San Jose, CA 95103

Santa Cruz Mineral & Gem Society
PO Box 343
Santa Cruz, CA 95061

Santa Lucia Rockhounds
PO Box 1672
Paso Robles, CA 93447

Santa Monica Gemological Society
PO Box 652
Santa Monica, CA 90404

Santa Rosa Mineral & Gem Society
PO Box 7036
Santa Rosa, CA 95407

Searcher Gem & Mineral Society
Box 3492
Anaheim, CA 92803

Searles Lake Gem & Mineral Society
PO Box 966
Trona, CA 93562

Sequoia Gem & Mineral Society
PO Box 1245
Redwood City, CA 94064

Sequoia Mineral Society
4954 North Del Mar
Fresno, CA 93704

Shadow Mountain Gem & Mineral
Society
PO Box 358
Cathedral City, CA 92234

Shasta Gem & Mineral Society
PO Box 424
Redding, CA 96099

Sierra Pelona Rock Club
PO Box 699
Newhall, CA 91321

South Bay Lapidary & Mineral
Society
PO Box 1606
Torrance, CA 90505

South Lake Tahoe Gem & Mineral
Society
PO Box 7186
S. Lake Tahoe, CA 96158

Southern California
Micromineralogists
4759 Blackthorne Ave.
Long Beach, CA 90808

Southern California Paleontological
Society
1826 Ninth St.
Manhattan Beach, CA 90266

Southwest Rockwranglers
1824 West Rosecrans
Gardena, CA 90249

Stockton Lapidary & Mineral Society
3136 East Anita
Stockton, CA 95205

Superior California Gem & Mineral
Association
PO Box 144
Chico, CA 95927

Sutter Buttes Gem & Mineral Society
PO Box 268
Marysville, CA 95901

Tehachapi Valley Gem & Mineral
Society
PO Box 4400-132
Tehachapi, CA 93561

Trinity Gem & Mineral Society
PO Box 159
Weaverville, CA 96093

Tule Gem & Mineral Society
PO Box 1061
Visalia, CA 93279

Vava Valley Gem & Mineral Society
PO Box 368
Vacaville, CA 95696

Vallejo Gem & Mineral Society
PO Box 389
Vallejo, CA 94589

Valley Gems
9050½ West Avenue J
Lancaster, CA 93536

Valley of the Moon Gem &
Mineral Club
PO Box 583
Sonoma, CA 95476

Valley Prospectors
PO Box 2923
San Bernardino, CA 92406

Ventura Gem & Mineral Society
PO Box 1573
Ventura, CA 93002

Victor Valley Gem & Mineral Club
15056 B Seventh St.
Victorville, CA 92307

VIP Gem & Mineral Society
7357 Hesperia Ave.
Reseda, CA 91335

Vista Gem & Mineral Society
PO Box 1641
Vista, CA 92083

W.L.A. Japanese American League
1928 Armacost Ave.
Los Angeles, CA 90025

West End Prospectors
PO Box 834
Fontana, CA 92335

Westside Mineralogists
1826 Ninth St.
Manhattan Beach, CA 90266

Whittier Gem & Mineral Society
PO Box 66
Whittier, CA 90608

Willits Gem & Mineral Club
4500 Canyon Rd.
Willits, CA 95490

Woodland Hills Rock Chippers
PO Box 205
Woodland, Hills, CA 91365

Yucaipa Valley Gem & Mineral
Society
PO Box 494
Yucaipa, CA 92399

INDEX

black with white or gray
banding, 190
blue-sheen, 193
gold-sheen, 193
gray, 187
gray with cream or silver
banding, 190
green-sheen, 192–93
mahogany, 187, 188, 191
rainbow, 187, 188, 192–93
red-and-black, 187, 188, 191
silver-and-gray, 187
silver-sheen, 193
obsidian needles, 191
Oceanview Mine, 21
Old Camp, 74–75
Old Toltec Mine, 114–15
onyx
beige, 103
honey and gray-banded, 101–3
opal
with chalcedony, 183
cherry, 100
common, 78, 83, 98–100,
123–25
green, 100, 125
orange, 100
precious, 118–20
red, 100
white, 100, 125
yellow, 100
Opal Hill Mine, 25–27, 28
opalite
black dendritic with white,
61–63
non-specific, 184
pink, 111, 112
pistachio green, 111, 112
rose pink, 64

white, 64
white with amber-colored
agate centers, 63
Opal Mountain, 98–100
Orocopia Mountains, 49–52

pahoehoe, 85–86
Palos Verdes Beach, 153–55
Patrick's Point Beach, 135–36
Patton's Training Field, 34, 35
Pebble Terrace, 26, 28–29
Peterson Mountain, 163–65
petrified whalebone, 139
petrified wood
agatized, 137–39, 186
black, 181–82
brown, 181–82
gray, 181–82
green, 125
light tan with cream or white
streaks, 181–82
non-specific, 106, 108, 121,
179–80, 202–4
red, 181–82
regulations and limits, 4
white, 125, 181–82
Pisgah Crater, 82, 84–88
Point Reyes Bird Observatory, 139
prehistoric sites
Early Man Site, 104
stone fortifications, 39
Price, George, 157
Providence Mountains, 72–73
psilomelane, 39–41, 46–48
Pulga, 173–74
pyrite, 72

quartz
asterated (cat's-eye), 131

About the Author

Gail A. Butler was born in California, as were her parents. This in itself is noteworthy, since not many people were actually born in California, most having imported themselves.

Gail has been a rockhound all her life and continually works to improve her lapidary skills, as well as discover new areas to collect rocks and minerals. She is also an avid and successful gold prospector who spends many weekends panning and sluicing cold mountain streams or metal detecting dry mountain washes for that elusive golden metal for which California is so well known.

An avid explorer and accomplished wilderness camper, she has spent much time prospecting for rocks, minerals, gold, and lost treasure in the deserts and mountains of California.

Gail learned many of her skills and interests from her grandfather, a prospector who hunted for gold and other precious metals, uranium, and minerals. She is passing this legacy on to her nephew, Perry Butler, who, at the age of eleven, is already an accomplished rockhound and gold prospector, as well as a published author.

Gail is a contributing editor to *Rock & Gem* magazine and has written many articles on rockhounding, gold prospecting, lapidary, and other subjects for this and other publications. One of her most unusual writing experiences occurred when she was asked to write an article on dowsing for a Greek publication, *News on Minerals*. When a copy of the published article was sent to her, she was unable to read a word of it. It was truly Greek to her!

She recently retired from the Los Angeles County Sheriff's Department, where she worked as a deputy sheriff for twenty years.

Gail plans and departs for her adventures, explorations, and expeditions from her home in Upland, California.

About the California Federation of Mineralogical Societies

The California Federation of Mineralogical Societies (CFMS) is a nonprofit, educational organization founded in 1936 to bring about a closer association of clubs and societies devoted to the study of earth sciences and the practice of lapidary arts in the western United States. The CFMS includes over 130 societies located in California, Arizona, and Nevada, and provides services to its member societies in the areas of education, insurance coverage, field trips, lapidary workshops, contests of various sorts, youth activities including a badge program, and more. It annually awards scholarships to deserving students pursuing college degrees within the earth sciences. The CFMS also sponsors an annual show in affiliation with one or more of its member societies. Together with six other regional federations, the CFMS is a part of the national American Federation of Mineralogical Societies.